DEDICATION

This book is dedicated to my family and friends for their support and enthusiasm. I also thank the many talented bartenders, bar chefs, and mixologists around the world whose dedication and passion inspire me to celebrate the art, craft, and alchemy of a well-made cocktail.

ACKNOWLEDGMENTS

My journey through mixology would not be complete without working alongside, learning from, and sharing with my friends and colleagues in the beverage, food, and media industries. I am thrilled to share my recipes in this book. However, it would not be complete without a few classic recipes throughout, and the wonderful contributions from the respected contributors who shared their own concoctions within these pages. I give heartfelt thanks, admiration, and acknowledgment to the following industry experts: Cheryl Charming, Chris Milligan, Todd Walker, Andrew Roy, Alex Velez, Rick Dobbs, Jacqueline Patterson, Jacob Briars, Jason Williams, Jeffrey Morgenthaler, Philip Duff, Garrett Richard, Amit Gilad, H. Joseph Ehrmann, Allison Evanow, Erik Teckosky, Joao Eusebio, Victoria Damato-Moran, and Todd Richman, as well as Gary Regan for his "spirit"ual guidance in mixology and mindful bartending.

Many thanks to Claire Barrett Photography whose incredible photography brings the recipes to life throughout the book, and to Gabriella Marks for her author headshot.

Thank you also to Danielle Chiotti who got this project sailing into the hands of the wonderful publishing team at Adams Media.

CONTENTS

Introduction 10

CHAPTER 1: **Mixology Basics** 13

CHAPTER 2: **Garden to Glass** 31

CHAPTER 3: **Grape to Glass** 57

CHAPTER 5: Mixing It Up: Infusions, Meat, Dairy, Eggs, Liqueurs, and Bitters 121

CHAPTER 6: Mixers, Garnishes, and Ice 155

INTRODUCTION

Upscale, local ingredients are gracing menus across the country but you won't just find them traveling from farm to table. Those same fresh ingredients —free range eggs, seasonal fruits and veggies, and home-grown herbs—are also finding their way from garden to glass in the form of edible cocktails, gourmet libations inspired by your garden or local farmers' market.

A well-crafted cocktail, like a well-crafted dish, is one that is balanced on the palate; pleasing to the eye; and made from wholesome, quality ingredients. So, growing the ingredients in your own garden gives you the opportunity to know exactly what's going into your drink—as well as the satisfaction of creating your cocktail all the way from seedling to first sip. This book will guide you through planting, cooking, and mixing your edible cocktails, whether you're plucking fresh mint from your own herb garden or buying buckets of seasonal berries from the farmers' market.

The delicious recipes throughout this book include must-know classics and market-fresh modern creations from my arsenal of seasonally inspired concoctions. I'm also excited to share drinks from world-class bartenders and mixologists shaking it up around the globe. But in *Edible Cocktails*, you'll find more than just drinks. Here, you'll also learn how to incorporate dairy-, egg-, and meat-based infusions into your mixology; make your own liqueurs, syrups, jams, and purées; choose quality mixers; and create appropriate garnishes. If you're new to the world of cocktails, you'll also find some basic mixology tips and information on spirits, wines, bar tools, and glassware that will help you build your own sipping arena.

Whether you want to learn how to become a better bartender for your own cocktail parties or you want to experience the journey of creating a cocktail from planting to pouring, this book will teach you how to put both thought and care into what you drink as well as elevate your cocktails to new earth-friendly, culinary-focused, health-conscious heights. So raise your glass and toast the delectable bounty of edible cocktails!

CHAPTER 1

mixology basics

THE TREND TOWARD MARRYING THE KITCHEN AND THE BAR HAS ALREADY BEEN UNDERWAY FOR OVER A DECADE IN MIXOLOGY-FOCUSED BARS ACROSS THE GLOBE as well as in the homes of "foodies" and "cocktail geeks" worldwide. You can also incorporate the delicious, fresh foods that you love to eat into the lip-smacking cocktails that you drink. But in order to fully utilize the recipes and concepts in this book, you must start with a few tools and a few basic philosophies. From kitchen tools and glassware to special ingredients and liquors to kick-start your home bar, here you'll learn which home bar staples you need to start mixing your own edible cocktails. Stocking up can be the perfect opportunity to start scouring your favorite home stores, cooking websites, and even antique stores for intriguing cocktail shakers, fancy glasses, and vintage bar tools. Obviously, you can buy what you need according to your budget. Whether you choose high-end vintage stores or hunt through your neighborhood flea markets, Goodwill, or Salvation Army for little treasures, collecting cool pieces can become a passion. And, if there happens to be a wedding or special birthday in your future, adding beautiful barware to your wish list or registry will help you get a superb collection all the faster.

It All Begins in the Kitchen

Since edible cocktails incorporate many homemade ingredients, your everyday kitchen appliances will come in handy when you're ready to mix things up. You'll find that many of the recipes for jams, syrups, and so on require a certain amount of prep work before you're able to mix these items into your cocktail and to do this prep work you need to have the right tools on hand. For example, the same saucepan you may use to heat up soup for dinner is integral to making a fruity jam that can be shaken into a cocktail. Here, you'll find a list of everyday things that will come in handy when preparing the recipes on the coming pages. You likely already have most of these items, so it won't be difficult to get started.

○ **BLENDER OR FOOD PROCESSOR:** Either one can be used for blending, or mixing beverages, or grinding and finely chopping garnishes, etc.

○ **CUTTING BOARD:** You'll be doing a lot of chopping and peeling so make sure you have a good-sized cutting board. Although wood may be more aesthetically pleasing, bamboo or synthetic materials often are easier to clean as they are less porous and have fewer nooks and crannies in which bacteria can linger. Always clean your board often and scour it well.

○ **PARING KNIFE:** A good knife is a great investment for both cooking and cocktails. In fact, you should have at least two quality knives: one for slicing small fruits and one for chopping and cutting larger produce and food items.

○ **PEELER:** This will be used for peeling citrus zest to create "rounds" and strips for garnishes as well as taking the skins off fruits and veggies for juicing.

○ **GRATER:** Specialty cooking stores will carry small graters that are ideal for grating ginger, nutmeg, chocolate, citrus peel, etc. However, if you already have a box grater, that can work as well.

○ **WIRE SIEVE:** This small wire kitchen strainer with the diameter of a coffee mug is the same type of strainer that you likely use for cooking. In mixology this sieve is used in conjunction with the wire bar strainer when pouring drinks that have been shaken with muddled fruit and citrus. This practice, referred to as double straining, holds back the extra bits of fruit flesh and pulp that would otherwise end up floating around in the cocktail glass.

○ **CHEESECLOTH:** Cheesecloth, a gauze-like piece of cloth found at cooking stores, is used for slow straining and comes in handy for various recipes in this book when you want to vigilantly strain out any very fine solids while collecting liquids.

○ **ICE CUBE TRAYS:** Ice is integral to a quality cocktail, whether you're shaking, stirring, or serving a drink on the rocks. Buy ice cube trays with the largest openings you can find; these trays will produce large, solid ice cubes that are best both for shaking cocktails and for cooling drinks because they melt more slowly, thereby watering down the drink less quickly. For the same reason, margarine tubs, muffin tins, and other larger-than-usual ice cube molds are also helpful if you are making punches or sangrias. Some specialty stores and websites carry ice-sphere molds (almost tennis ball-sized ice balls), which have become all the rage in fancy cocktail bars.

○ **JUICER:** This is essential for juicing pineapples, apples, melons, cucumbers, carrots, etc. If you can afford a fancy one with all the bells and whistles, go for it! The higher-end juicers tend to come with sharper blades and make juicing quicker and easier than the cheaper ones. However, if a simple juicer fits your budget, that's fine, too. But if you go this route, it may be helpful to cut the fruit or veggies a bit smaller than usual as the blades may not be as big or sharp as the more professional juicers.

○ **MEASURING CUPS:** You'll need these for measuring bigger batch punches, sangrias, etc. The types of measuring cups you use for cooking are perfect. If you're making several ingredients or punches at a time, it would be convenient to have a one-cup measure and a larger one, such as a four-cup measure, on hand. Measuring spoons can also come in handy for smaller amounts.

○ **SAUCEPANS:** Small to medium-sized pans are ideal for syrups, depending on the quantities you intend to make. A large one, or even a double boiler, is helpful for making jams and purées.

○ **CLEAR BOTTLES AND JARS:** You will soon be making your own syrups, infusions, liqueurs, jams, and preserved fruits and veggies. So you will need vessels in which to store them. Start collecting reusable clear bottles (such as white wine bottles) for syrups and liqueurs. Jam jars can be found at many supermarkets or professional kitchen supply stores. Also keep your eyes open for beautiful, sealable, vintage glassware as these colorful, fresh ingredients are lovely to display as well as consume.

Stock Your Pantry

Don't be surprised if you start to see your kitchen and its contents in a whole new way when approaching cocktail-making with garden-fresh edibles in mind. Inspiration can strike at any time, so keeping some basic items on hand allows you to whip up an intoxicating creation on demand. The list below provides the building blocks for incorporating edible cocktails into any special meal or celebration, at any time.

- **SUGARS:** Try to keep granulated white, raw, brown, and powdered icing sugars on hand as various drinks, garnishes, or homemade ingredients call for different kinds of sugars. Most basic syrups and jams, for example, call for plain, old, granulated white sugar; however, mojitos, for example, take on a more authentic—and flavorful—taste with raw sugar syrup versus plain white sugar syrup. All types of sugar can be used for rimming, but icing (or powdered) sugar creates a tasty, decorative rim on a cocktail glass and having colored and flavored sugars in your cupboards allows for spontaneous creativity.

- **PECTIN:** Pectin is a setting agent, used particularly in some jelly recipes. You can make your own (see recipe in Chapter 4) or you can buy pectin in powdered or liquid form from the store.

- **CINNAMON STICKS:** Cinnamon sticks may be ground with sugar to use in rimmers or may be called for to flavor syrups, etc. The sticks will stay fresh for ages if kept in a small airtight jar.

- **WHOLE CLOVES:** These tiny baubles of pungent flavor can be ground or cooked whole to add a bit of spice to syrups and jams that may be shaken into your cocktails. Cloves (as well as nutmeg, cinnamon, and allspice) bring a wonderful aroma to holiday drinks in particular. One whiff of them in mulled wine or baked into a cake and it smells like a cozy Christmastime celebration.

- **NUTMEG:** Whole nutmeg is walnut size and can be stored for a long time in a sealable container. Grating fresh nutmeg over a cocktail gives it both an interesting look as well as an appetizing aroma and taste. You can also buy ground nutmeg if you prefer to skip the step of grating it yourself.

- **EGGS:** Eggs may seem like an odd cocktail ingredient if you are not yet familiar with drink recipes calling for them, but you'll want to have eggs on hand after you learn about their applications. Fresher farmers' market eggs are a great choice over supermarket ones which may have been sitting on shelves for a while. If you can only get to the store, look for hormone-free eggs. You want to incorporate healthier food items into mixology, so carry that philosophy through to each ingredient whenever possible.

○ **MILK AND CREAM:** Some classic recipes such as a Brandy Alexander or Grasshopper call for cream; however, milk can be substituted if you're watching your fat intake. Other recipes call specifically for milk. To ensure a healthier, quality culinary approach buy organic or hormone free, if possible.

○ **SALT:** Various kinds of salts are used for cooking and cocktails. Once in a while, a cocktail recipe may actually call for a pinch of salt, which is more than likely the normal table salt you probably already have on hand. However, kosher salt is great for rimming a margarita, for example. Or, you can get more gourmet by using pink Himalayan salt, smoked sea salt, or other fancy salts found at high-end grocers and specialty food stores.

○ **VINEGAR:** Vinegar may seem like an odd ingredient for a cocktail, but a little balsamic, red wine, or rice vinegar can bring a dynamic zing to cocktails. Learn more in the "shrubs" section.

○ **FRESH HERBS:** Herbs are often used in edible cocktails and if you are not growing your own, hit the farmers' market or your grocery store produce aisle. Start out by stocking up on the basics, including fresh mint, basil, and sage. Learn more about herbs in Chapter 2.

○ **SEASONAL FRUITS AND VEGGIES:** You'll want to have fruits and veggies on hand to muddle into a cocktail shaker, or to use in making fresh juices, garnishes, syrups, jams, etc. Grow your own varieties or explore local farmers' markets to find out what is in season.

○ **SEASONAL EDIBLE FLOWERS:** Edible flowers are commonly seen in gourmet salads and as decoration on plates, but they also make lovely garnishes for cocktails. Not all flowers are edible, of course, so the safest bet is to buy packages marked "edible flowers" at the store (usually found in the fresh herb section of gourmet grocers). Some farmers' market purveyors also have edible flowers for sale. Grow your own or see what local gardeners have in season.

○ **CITRUS:** Limes, lemons, oranges, grapefruits, kumquats, and yuzu are all options as juices, garnishes, and bases in homemade ingredients and infusions.

Basic Bar Tools

Now that you've stocked your kitchen with basic cooking tools and fresh ingredients, it's time to deck out your home bar. The good news is that you don't need many tools to make great cocktails. You can find most of the following items in gourmet cooking stores, at your local grocery or liquor store, or anywhere kitchen or bar equipment is sold. While you can get many of these pieces relatively inexpensively, feel free to splurge on some upscale showpieces. For example, some barware and glassware is so pretty, you may even wish to display it on a bookshelf in your living room. Particularly if you are hunting for one-of-a-kind items with which to build your bar, show off those decorative conversation starters!

○ **COCKTAIL SHAKER:** These can be fun or functional, and occasionally both. However, a Boston Shaker is the professional's choice. It is essentially a pint-sized glass with a metal tin that fits snugly over it. Many bartenders like to use this kind of shaker because they can build the drink in the glass part, which allows them and their guests to see the ingredients and quantities going into the drink. Once filled with ice, the tin is a great indicator of how cold the drink is because the temperature is easily felt through the metal and it becomes frosty, creating a visual cue, too.

○ **MUDDLER:** This can be made of wood, plastic, stone, or metal. It is essentially a pestle with a long handle to reach the bottom of a cocktail shaker. Use one to squash fruits, vegetables, and herbs in the bottom of the mixing glass, thereby releasing the juices, oils, and flavors of those ingredients.

○ **STRAINERS:** Cocktail strainers are different from the kitchen sieves and strainers described in the previous section. These are designed specifically to fit over the mouth of the cocktail shaker in order to hold back ice and fruit or herb particles while straining the liquid from the shaker into the cocktail glass. When "double straining" the cocktail strainer is used as usual, on the cocktail shaker. However, a small kitchen sieve is used in conjunction with it by straining from the shaker, into a wire sieve held directly over the cocktail glass. This ensures that any extra bits of solid ingredients that may have slipped through the cocktail strainer will be kept out of the glass.

> **HAWTHORNE STRAINER:** This kind of wire strainer is used in conjunction with the metal part of the Boston Shaker. It is usually metal and about the diameter of the glass. It has a coil around the perimeter, and holds back ice and other bits of fruit or solid ingredients from streaming into the glass tin after shaking ingredients in the shaker.

> **JULEP STRAINER:** This kind of strainer fits inside the glass part of the cocktail shaker. It is a slightly domed metal circle and has holes in it to allow liquid through. It

is used to hold back the ice after stirring a drink. The julep strainer has also been used to hold back the crushed ice when drinking (you guessed it) mint juleps.

○ **CITRUS PRESS:** This handheld device is shaped like half an orange, lemon, or lime, and it will become your new best friend when you're mixing up a cocktail that calls for fresh citrus juice. To use it, slice the fruit in half, place it cut-side down (where the holes are) then squeeze it directly over the mixing glass. This press makes getting out as much juice as possible a quicker and easier task than squeezing with your fingers or other tools.

○ **BAR SPOON:** This has a very long stem and measures about the same amount as a teaspoon. It is used for stirred drinks such as a classic martini or Manhattan.

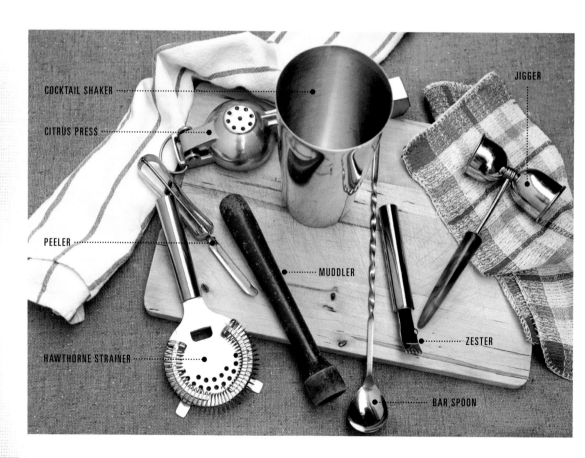

COCKTAIL SHAKER

CITRUS PRESS

PEELER

HAWTHORNE STRAINER

MUDDLER

BAR SPOON

ZESTER

JIGGER

○ **JIGGER:** A jigger is a tool used to measure the amount of alcohol poured into a drink by ounces or milliliters. You can find plastic ones that have the measurements printed directly onto them. However, the most common ones are metal and look like two cones connected back to back. One cone is larger (usually twice the size) of the smaller one. It is helpful to keep at least two of these jiggers on hand, one that is 1½ ounces × ¾ ounce, and one that is 1 ounce × ½ ounce, as some drinks may call for varying measures. Sometimes people use shot glasses (which typically measure 1 ounce) in place of a jigger.

○ **ICE SCOOP:** You will be surprised how often this comes in handy. Even for home parties, an ice scoop is more appetizing than using your fingers or fiddling with ice tongs to fill a cocktail shaker or glass.

Rule of Thumb . . .

Stir drinks with ice when they are all liquor. This cools them without over-diluting them from melting ice, and also avoids them getting "cloudy" from shaking. However, vigorously shake then strain cocktails when they have citrus, dairy, egg, or other ingredients that need to be well mixed.

GLASSWARE: THE MOST IMPRESSIVE GARNISH

When you see a beautiful dish placed on a lovely table setting, doesn't it make you more excited for the meal you are about to enjoy? In the same way, when you're ready to enjoy a cocktail, the glass is an important part of the presentation of a great drink. Some kinds of cocktails are glass specific, too. You wouldn't serve a mojito in a champagne flute, or champagne in a bar mug—it wouldn't make sense. Gathering the appropriate glassware is another fun—and addictive—pastime for the professional and amateur cocktail enthusiast. And, after all the effort you're putting into building your edible cocktails, it makes sense to make your drinks shine in the most perfect presentation possible. So have the following types of glassware on hand:

- **CHAMPAGNE FLUTE:** A long, narrow glass used for sparkling wines, and sparkling cocktails (champagne coupes—rounded, shallower glasses—were popular in years gone by, but aren't used much today).

- **COCKTAIL:** Any smallish, unusual, aesthetically pleasing glass used for cocktails (catch-all term for cool glassware you find in random places).

- **COLLINS:** Typically, a collins glass is narrow and tall.

- **JULEP CUP:** These decorative metal cups are used specifically for Mint Juleps, and were popularized at the Kentucky Derby. The metal becomes very frosty when the cup is filled with crushed ice.

- **MARGARITA:** A wide-rimmed, bowl-shaped glass used specifically for margaritas.

- **MARTINI (COCKTAIL):** V-shaped cocktail glass known as the martini glass; not only martinis are served in it, but every variation of "tini" drink you can think of (also traditionally called a "cocktail" glass among mixology purists . . . so don't let that throw you).

- **BAR MUG:** A thick, glass mug that is used for beer when chilled, but is also heat-resistant for hot toddies when serving warm drinks.

- **ROCKS:** A short glass used for sipping whiskey or other drinks typically served "on the rocks," or "over ice."

- **SHOT:** A 1-ounce glass that can be used to measure a 1-ounce pour in a cocktail.

- **WINE, RED:** A rounded, bowl-shaped glass with a large surface area allowing for more oxygen to react with the wine, thereby allowing the flavors and aromas to "open."

- **WINE, WHITE:** A smaller, more tulip-shaped wine glass usually associated with white wine. Chill the glassware when serving cold drinks such as white, sweet, or rosé wine.

- **DECANTER:** Usually used for expensive red wines that react well with a bit of oxygen before drinking. When you let a wine "breathe" before serving, it is usually poured into a decanter and allowed to sit for 15–30 minutes (sometimes longer) before being served.

- **WINE BUCKET:** It's not a bad idea to have a wine bucket that you can fill with ice and a bit of cold water to keep your white wine (or chilled vodka) cold when entertaining.

Stocking Your Home Bar

Now for the fun part! While you are growing (or shopping for) and cooking up your own ingredients to make edible cocktails, you will need to stock the liquor with which to mix them. You may already have a favorite spirit—or think you do—but as you experiment with different cocktail recipes and start to create your own, you might discover that you actually like tequila, or gin, or whiskey . . . or whatever you may *not* be accustomed to drinking. Mixology, like cooking, is about creativity and exploration and the more options you have on hand, the more favorites you can discover!

Stocking your home bar may be expensive, but you can do it in increments. Start with a bottle of each of the basics, and then expand your liquor collection over time. Once you get into mixology and cocktail making, you will enjoy sharing and showing off the interesting products you accumulate.

START WITH SPIRITS

Alcohol is made when a grain, vegetable, fruit, or sugar product is fermented with yeast. This process creates a kind of beer that is then put through a still (distillation machine) where the fermented liquid is heated, evaporated, and cooled and the remaining droplets collected. Spirits, or distilled alcohol, are the result of this process. Sometimes that newly created alcohol is distilled a second (or more) time to further remove impurities. This is why some bottles read "triple distilled," for example.

Multiple Distillations

Keep in mind that just because an alcohol claims to be distilled many times, doesn't necessarily mean that it's a better product. Each time a liquor is distilled, it loses some of the characteristics and flavor of the original fermented mixture. By distilling something over and over, is the distiller looking to create a purer product, which can be a good thing depending on what he or she is going for in the final liquor? Or, is the distiller trying to mask a lower-quality product by stripping out as much of the original character as possible? That's not to suggest that products claiming to be distilled multiple times are bad, but be aware that if a marketing campaign claims that multiple distillation leads to a better end product, it's not always true.

Once the liquid has gone through the distillation process, it is very high-proof alcohol, and not fit for consumption. Therefore, the next step is to dilute it with water, which not only works to bring down the alcohol ratio and make the spirit consumable for humans but also helps to make the spirit ultimately more palatable. After dilution with water, the spirit is sometimes aged in wood in order for it to become richer and mellower. During this time, the spirits will also pull color and flavor characteristics from the barrels. Here are some of the main spirits that you will find in the recipes in this book and that you want to have stocked in your home bar:

○ **VODKA:** Although vodka is technically defined as "a colorless, odorless neutral spirit," any connoisseur will tell you that there are slight differences between vodkas made from wheat (creamier), rye (spicier), grapes (slightly sweeter), and so on. Try a blind taste test of vodkas made from different materials on your own and see if you can tell the difference.

○ **GIN:** In the most simplistic definition, we could say that gin is juniper-infused vodka because in order to be classified as gin, the base spirit must be infused with juniper, at least. Beyond that, distillers use everything from citrus peels, to spices, to vegetables and flowers to create interesting flavors in their products. You may see terms such as "London dry gin," which is quite common and means that the spirit is juniper- and citrus-heavy, and contains no added sugars, etc. You may also have heard of sloe gin, which is essentially more of a liqueur than a traditional gin. It is sweet and infused with sloe berries, which are somewhat like a small plum, or damson.

○ **RUM:** Typically made from molasses, rum can be light (unaged) or dark (aged in wood from which it gets additional flavor and color). There is also spiced rum, which means that it's infused with spices like cinnamon, or caramel, or other herbs. Rum has become very popular over the last few years, so there are many new brands becoming available worldwide.

○ **CACHAÇA:** This spirit is essentially Brazilian rum, although cachaça makers like to distinguish themselves from the rum category by pointing out that this liquor is made from fermented sugarcane juice versus molasses. Some of those companies are also seeking to establish that in order to be called cachaça, the alcohol must be made in Brazil, which is what French wine makers have done with Champagne.

○ **TEQUILA:** The best quality tequila is made 100 percent from Mexican blue agave, a succulent plant in the lily family. *Blanco* or silver means the tequila is still clear in the bottle and has been aged very little, if at all. *Reposado* means the tequila has rested in a wood barrel for two to six months. *Añejo* means aged, and that this spirit has probably been in wood up to a year. A relatively new term "extra añejo" means the tequila could be aged at least three years in wood. (Everyone has their own preference but I like to use silver for tequila cocktails other than margaritas, reposado for margaritas because they add a bit of extra depth to the drink, and the añejos to sip on their own from a brandy snifter, as one would a fine cognac.)

○ **WHISKEY:** If you are a whiskey drinker, chances are that you are pretty particular about what you like—and you should be—as the different kinds of whiskeys are quite distinct from one another:

> **Bourbon** must be made with from at least 51 percent corn in the United States (usually in Kentucky) and aged for at least two years in new, charred American oak barrels.

Scotch is made with malted barley in Scotland. There are many different types of Scotch, too, for those wanting to seek out and learn more.

Rye whiskey, as the name suggests, is made from rye and has a bit of a dry, spicy kick to it. It's specifically called for in some classic cocktail recipes!

Irish whiskey must be made in Ireland and must be aged for three years in wood barrels.

Canadian whiskey, as you probably have guessed, comes from Canada. It is made from many blended grains but rye is particularly prominent.

○ **BRANDY:** A distilled spirit made from grapes. The most famous of this category is probably cognac, which is made in a specific region in France. Brandy de Jerez is made in Spain, and pisco is sometimes referred to as a "South American brandy," made mainly in Peru and Chile.

"Whiskey" or "Whisky"?

If you are confused as to how the word should be spelled, here is a little clue: If there is no "e," "whisky" is usually referring to Scotch. "Whiskey" with an "e" can refer to all other whiskeys, particularly ones made in the United States, such as bourbon.

SOME OTHER BAR ESSENTIALS

In addition to spirits, many cocktails also call for additional ingredients. These are used to complement, round out, and contrast with or further enhance the base spirit, all of which result in out-of-this-world drinks with layers of flavor. This book provides recipes to make some of these items yourself using some of your favorite fruits and spices, and certainly, you could go crazy with a long list of fun things to mix into your drinks. However, here are a few simple suggestions to enhance your bar.

○ **VERMOUTH:** A fortified wine (some distillate has been added) used in several classic recipes, such as the classic martini and Manhattan. Keep a bottle of both dry vermouth (a relatively dry, white wine-based fortified wine used in martinis, for example) and sweet vermouth (a slightly sweeter, red wine–based fortified wine) on hand. Be sure to store them in the refrigerator; as with all wine, even when chilled, vermouth can go bad within a week.

○ **LIQUEURS:** Whether fruity, flowery, creamy, coffee-flavored, nutty, minty or chocolaty, liqueurs are lovely to serve chilled either on their own (perhaps after a dinner party) or mixed into cocktails. See Chapter 5 for some recipes to make your own liqueurs.

○ **BITTERS:** These flavor-enhancers should be thought of as the "salt" of cocktails. Just as a pinch of salt brings zing to a soup, pasta, or other dish, a dash of bitters boosts flavors in a cocktail. Keep a bottle each of Angostura and Peychaud's on hand, and experiment with some of the flavored bitters that have hit the market over the past several years.

○ **ORGEAT:** This almond syrup is called for in several classic cocktail recipes such as the mai tai, and is commonly found in liquor stores.

○ **FALERNUM:** A spicy, tropical syrup used in rum-based, tropical tiki drinks as well as other creative recipes. This can be found in specialty stores or online.

○ **ORANGE FLOWER WATER:** This fragrant orange blossom–infused water is often found in ethnic food stores.

○ **ROSE WATER:** Keep a bottle of potable rose water at your bar as a dash will enhance many a floral or fruity cocktail.

○ **TABASCO:** This hot sauce is fantastic in Bloody Marys as well as other spicy concoctions.

○ **GARNISHES:** These are covered more extensively in Chapter 6, but to get started, keep these key garnishes on hand: lemons, limes, oranges, cherries, onions, and olives. Additional garnishes can include candied ginger or citrus peel, edible flowers, lemongrass stalks, and other seasonal fruits and vegetables.

Not Every Mixed Drink Is a Cocktail

Now that you've started to become a cocktail aficionado, the next step is to understand the drinks themselves. These days, people worldwide use the term "cocktail" for almost anything with alcohol in it, so it may surprise you to learn that a cocktail is merely one classification of mixed drink. Below is a bevy of boozy combinations, the correct terms for them, and the basic rules of thumb that you need to create them:

○ **COBBLER**: Spirit or wine + sugar over crushed ice, often garnished with fruit.

○ **COCKTAIL**: Spirit + sugar + water (can be ice) + bitters.

○ **DAISY**: Spirit + liqueur + citrus.

○ **FIZZ**: Similar to the sour (2 parts spirit, 1 part sweet, 1 part sour) with added club soda and optional egg variations.

○ **FLIP**: Spirit + sherry + egg + sugar.

○ **PUNCH**: One rule of thumb for punch is: spirit + spice + sugar + citrus + water (or tea). Can also have this ratio: 1 part sour + 2 parts sweet + 3 parts strong (spirit) + 4 parts weak (mixer).

○ **SOUR**: Spirit + citrus + sugar. Generally the ratio is 2 parts spirit + 1 part each sour (citrus) and sugar.

○ **SMASH**: Spirit + fruit and/or herb + sugar + citrus built in the tall glass it is served in.

○ **SWIZZLE**: Spirit + lime + bitters + sugar + crushed ice built in the tall glass it is served in and vigorously stirred (swizzled) until the outside of the glass is frosted.

Now, after gathering some basic knowledge about edible cocktails and general mixology, you have been inspired to stock your pantry, start a cocktail-ware collection, and begin building your arsenal of spirits and other bar essentials that you'll need to have a fun and functional home bar. However, before we go any further, let's take some time to think about where the market-fresh cocktail "garden to glass" concept begins—in the ground. Before you start mixing, you can start growing, or learning where to source, fresh-from-the-earth ingredients. The next chapter will guide you through planting, sourcing, shopping, and using herbs, fruits, veggies, and flowers that will enhance not only your cocktails, but your day-to-day approach to eating and drinking.

CHAPTER 2

GaRdeN to GLass

THERE'S SOMETHING SATISFYING ABOUT GROWING YOUR OWN FOOD. FROM THE TIME WE ARE CHILDREN, WE REVEL IN THE SATISFACTION OF CREATING something beautiful. By actually touching the soil, interacting with it, and producing herbs, fruits, and flowers that please your eyes *and* your palate as well, everything just seems to taste better—including a cocktail! After all, what makes a dining or drinking experience more sensual than having guided the ingredients every step of the way from garden to glass?

In this chapter, you'll learn everything you need to know about growing the fruits and veggies that will eventually end up being muddled, jammed, puréed, and mixed into your edible cocktails: What should you grow? Should you compost? How can you create your own cocktail garden? You don't have to live in a rural setting to get growing. Even if you're living in a small apartment in a city, you'll learn how you can bring a piece of the outdoors inside. And if you're not able to grow your own produce, you'll learn how to find what you're looking for—and how to get the most out of your local farmers' market. Anyone can put healthy, homegrown ingredients onto the tables and into the cocktail shakers. Let's get growing!

Plant Your Own Cocktail Garden

The first step in cultivating your culinary creativity is to actually plant your cocktail garden. If you are fortunate enough to have a lot of space and land, choose an area with both direct sun as well as some shady bits, if possible, so you can arrange your garden according to the needs of various plants. If you are a city dweller and find yourself glancing around your apartment thinking you don't have space to start a garden, guess again! You'll be surprised by what you can do with only a square foot or two of space. So let's take some time and figure out where you should prepare to plant.

A Perfect Pairing

The good news is that everything that is used in your edible cocktails can be used in cooking as well, so there is a double benefit—and no-brainer cocktail and food pairings. For example, with your homegrown basil, why not make a light lunch with fresh bread from your local bakery, a Caprese Salad (fresh tomato, basil, and mozzarella cheese) washed down with a Caprese Martini (see recipe in Chapter 7)?

IN YOUR BACKYARD

You know that exterior green carpet you spend hours seeding, watering, mowing, raking, and fussing over to keep it looking fresh? Yes, your lawn. Think about all the effort, money, water, and time used on a relatively useless patch of land. Sure, a lawn may look nice but it is not particularly functional. Why not take at least a portion of that space, rip up the grass, and create a cocktail garden?

Use large stones, bricks, large pieces of driftwood, or lumber from your local home-improvement store to create rings, squares, or other aesthetically pleasing spaces in which you can plant your veggies, herbs, fruits, and flowers. Prepare the earth for planting by digging up whatever was in there before (grass, weeds, etc.), and add some fertilizer, manure, or organic compost (see directions in this chapter to make your own compost). You may just find that getting yourself, or another family member, to water the yard may be a much easier and more fun task when the payoff is a delicious drink featuring your own fresh products.

Garden Decorating Tip

Collect interesting rocks, shells, and driftwood for your garden patch on family vacations or hiking trips. Not only are such items beautiful, natural, and free, but each item is a souvenir of a special place or day.

ON YOUR BALCONY

If you live in a city, you likely live in an apartment or condo. Space may be limited, and you don't necessarily have access to a patch of land. Don't lose heart! If you're lucky enough to have a balcony, you already have the next best thing.

Most balconies get direct sunlight for at least a couple of hours per day. And, they also get shade. And, certainly, your balcony receives a natural watering in the rainy season of whichever city you live in. With these almost-ideal growing conditions, you will be surprised by how quickly—and easily—your balcony can be bursting with green, leafy plants, colorful flowers, and aromatic herbs! To bring this natural beauty to your balcony purchase some earthen pots, wooden planters, or even half a wine barrel to house your urban garden. (Wine barrels can often be purchased at gardening stores or sometimes directly from a nearby winery.) Fill these with potting soil and edible plants and flowers, and you'll have brought both beauty and homegrown nutrition to your city dwelling.

If your balcony is a small one, think multi-dimensionally. If you don't have a large surface area, find (or make) growing boxes that are long and narrow, and hang them on a railing or fasten them to a wall or railing about 18 inches above one another. An old, narrow shelving unit from a thrift store is another good way to create a stacked balcony garden. Plants needing less light can be planted in lower boxes, and those craving sun can go into the upper ones. These kinds of planting boxes can be found at home-improvement stores.

You can also gather a few decorative bricks and lay them on their sides. The holes in the bricks can become lovely little homes for budding seedlings, which can later be transplanted into larger pots. Building-supply stores will have a variety of bricks from which to choose. You're better off buying the smaller, earth-colored bricks, which are small, pretty, and work well for

seedlings; the gray cinderblock bricks are a bit large for balcony growing and are better experimented with in a yard.

When you begin to utilize your balcony to grow plants that you will use in your kitchen and bar, you also create a pleasant space in which to relax, meditate, read a book, enjoy a morning coffee, and visit with friends. Plus, imagine how impressed your guests will be when they see you plucking fresh basil that you've grown yourself, and using it in a delicious cocktail a few seconds later right before their eyes.

WINDOWSILL

You may not think that a windowsill would give you much space for growing, but it is actually perfect for nurturing small plants. Herbs, a small chili plant, or a sweet-smelling pot of lavender can flourish in such a small space. The key with windowsills is to water often in summer if the box is in direct sunlight, and maybe even create some shade for it if the plants' leaves are turning brown or the pots are drying out very quickly. Thyme, rosemary, and sage do particularly well in very hot, dry spots, whereas mint flourishes in the shade. Because the soil is relatively shallow in this kind of container, using a liquid fertilizer every couple of weeks is also recommended, and transplanting into larger pots once the plants need more space is advised. Here is an important note: If the box is on the outside of your window, be sure to secure it very well so it does not pose a danger to those below!

Grow Some Design

Stop by your local wine shop or visit a winery to search for wooden wine boxes that you can use as windowsill planters. Drill a couple of holes in the bottom of the wooden box so that the soil can drain well. Reusing any kind of packaging is environmentally friendly, and the wood gives a hint of rural chic to a city dwelling, inside or outside the window.

IN YOUR HOUSE

If you don't have any outdoor space available, you can still grow some plants inside your house or apartment. A large pot can hold several types of herbs at once. Mint, basil, and rosemary would be a useful trio for many cooking and cocktail applications, for example. You can also optimize an empty corner of a room by thinking vertically. Filling a corner bookshelf with various pots or hanging a plant holder from the ceiling is a way to create a space for a tiny garden in just about any environment.

COMMUNITY GARDENS

If the thought of growing plants in your own living space truly seems like an impossibility, take a look around your town. Chances are that there are more options than you realize to fulfill your desire for self-grown produce. With a bit of gumption and research, you will find a solution!

Start by looking into community gardens in your area. Many cities as well as small towns reserve plots of land specifically for this purpose. A community garden is essentially a block or half block of space where locals can rent (or pay dues for) a small bit of land to grow their own veggies, fruits, flowers, and so on. Because supply is limited and demand is great, it is possible that you may be put on a waiting list to obtain your own little parcel of earth, but the wait is worth it. If you are particularly anxious to get started, get to know some of the people who already have one; they might be willing to share the work, the expense, and the bounty.

FORAGING IN THE WILD

If you're interested in procuring your produce in a more adventurous way, you may want to give foraging a try. After all, there is a certain romanticism in plucking fruits, herbs, flowers, and veggies out of the wild and taking them home to eat (or drink). However, if you decide to go this route, use caution and do plenty of research before you begin picking. Some towns have foraging groups and classes available for those looking to venture out with a guide or who seek some deeper knowledge before their first time gathering from the wild. It can become a wonderful hobby, so if you are interested, talk to foraging experts, read books on the subject, join a foraging group, and set off into the wild (or even after wild-growing items in your own surroundings) to gather a cornucopia of goodies for your edible cocktails. But be careful: If you're not familiar with a particular plant, keep in mind that it could be poisonous.

Start a Compost Pile

To get the most out of your garden, wherever you've decided to plant, you may want to consider starting a compost pile, a mound of decomposed organic matter used to fertilize plants. Organic matter can be anything from fruit peels to coffee grinds. It can also be broken down wood, leaves, or natural fabrics such as cotton. But creating your own compost takes time because the materials need to break down naturally (in other words, rot), and you will need to do a few things to help that process along. Like a fine dish or cocktail, making your own compost merely requires following a recipe. Granted, this recipe doesn't sound so appetizing to you but it will to your budding, hungry plants. And, just as there are varying levels of gardening, there are varying levels of composting as well.

START SMALL

If you are doing a simple, small, kitchen-counter compost, there isn't a whole lot to do. All you need is a jar or ceramic dish (preferably with a lid) and a little counter space. It really is that easy.

If you're a tea drinker, just throw your used tea leaves into the container and they'll naturally decompose. If you are more of a coffee drinker, you can use your old coffee grounds as well. Because coffee is more acidic, it works particularly well in dry soil. So if you live in an arid climate, collect your coffee grounds and sprinkle them on your rose bushes, and edible garden or decorative plants.

If you want to get more industrious with your kitchen compost, throw in fruit and veggie scraps, old bread, and pretty much anything left over from a meal except meat. If you choose to go this far with your home compost, it would be best to use a larger container with a sealable lid. You may also consider moving this kind of more extensive compost outside, though, because as the items inside the container break down, they can emit an unpleasant smell and attract insects, such as fruit flies and ants.

GO BIG

If you want to create a larger compost pile outside, which is pretty necessary if you are undertaking organic gardening, you can do this too; it just takes a bit more work. Nowadays, there are a lot of options when it comes to outdoor compost bins. You can build your own bin from wood, if that fits with the décor and philosophy of your garden. However, you can also buy a plethora of plastic bins and tools to help your composting efforts. You can even use something as simple as a large, outdoor garbage can. You can also buy compost "tumblers" which are round and affixed to a metal frame. You can fill these with compost, and then spin them around to mix the contents well.

Keep It Wet

Don't forget to water and stir your compost regularly—weekly is a good rule of thumb—but adjust to the needs of your compost pile. It should not get bone dry nor soaking wet, but rather stay slightly moist most of the time.

If you have a large garden, consider working with a good-sized compost bin, into which you can throw everything from raked leaves, to wood bark, to cardboard, to kitchen scraps. In addition to collecting the materials for the compost pile, you will need to add water from time to time, and stir the mixture to oxygenate it. Buy some worms to help speed the process along (worms and maggots may show up voluntarily but if you don't get enough you can purchase them at gardening stores and fishing tackle stores). The worm's role in composting is to eat through the matter in your bin, thereby aerating it and moving little bits around in the process. (They are essentially helping you stir the compost.) And, like all living creatures, what they eat is excreted later. This worm poop is also good fertilizer for your garden.

It can take up to a year for an outdoor compost pile to become ready for use. If you don't want to wait that long, it's helpful to start off your compost pile with a borrowed bucketful from a friend who already has some mature compost that contains plenty of bacteria and worms already at work.

Why go to all this trouble, you ask? Well, if you are truly passionate about this kind of gardening, it is rewarding to be part of the process every step of the way. It's also a great, environmentally friendly way of getting rid of waste. Rather than throwing all that unwanted stuff into garbage bags, which wind up in landfills, you can use leftover food, unwanted natural-fiber clothes, raked leaves, and so on, to fertilize the ground to grow healthful, organic food to nourish your family, friends, and soul. (If this all sounds like a bit more than you bargained for, there is nothing wrong with buying compost or fertilizer at gardening stores, by the way!)

Collect Rainwater

If you have enough space, and are in a rainy enough environment, collecting rainwater is a wonderful way to hydrate your plants. Whether inside or outside, your plants need plenty of water, and Mother Nature does not follow your watering schedule! Therefore, collecting extra water for indoor and outdoor watering is a good idea. It's free, it's natural, and it comes without the added chemicals that are often included in tap water.

A plastic-lined, wooden wine barrel or plastic tub would work well in a garden or yard (place it under the rain gutter of your house to get the most from every downpour). In an apartment, you can also put big pots on your balcony to collect a gray sky's offerings. A large jar on a windowsill could also manage to get a rainy day treat for your little sprouts. For people in warm, humid climates, keep in mind that stagnant water can attract bugs and mosquitoes, so use the water as you get it, or cover it and use it within a week or so of collecting it.

If collecting rainwater isn't an option in your climate (or simply isn't functional for your lifestyle), then try to use the same water on your plants that you would drink yourself. After all, you're going to all this effort to grow your own healthful ingredients, so why not pay attention to using the best quality ingredients every step of the way? Distilled water can be a good option or, if you filter your own drinking water using a self-filtering jug, that would work just as well.

What to Grow

So, now that you know how to grow your own ingredients, it's time to take a look at what you should plant. Of course, where you live may have an influence on this decision. If you're living in a tropical area, you will have access to things that those living in cold climates may not. Here you'll find a relatively universal suggestion list of commonly used cooking and cocktail herbs, flowers, fruits, and veggies. Whether you are starting with a few pots on a windowsill or an acre of farmable land, you will find some plants that will fit with your geographic location, your level of gardening prowess, and your personal palate.

ESSENTIAL HERBS AND SPICES

Herbs are integral to creating culinary cocktails. Whether muddled, made into syrups, infused directly into spirits, or used as garnish, these plants, with their aromas and flavors, bring the freshness of the earth to the cocktail glass. Here is a list of suggestions as to where to begin, but as you get more excited about growing your own cocktail garden, you can expand this list as far as your local nursery, farmers' market, or green thumb will take you!

○ **SPEARMINT:** A cross between peppermint and watermint and is delicious muddled into cocktails such as Mojitos.

○ **PEPPERMINT:** Great for teas, syrups.

○ **APPLEMINT:** Has a strong herbal quality, good for mint jelly.

○ **PINEAPPLE MINT:** Fruity aromatics.

○ **CHOCOLATE MINT:** Great with dark spirits.

○ **THAI BASIL:** Strong licorice flavor.

○ **LEMON BASIL:** Fresh lemony flavor.

○ **CINNAMON BASIL:** Imparts a spicy, cinnamon flavor.

○ **GENOVESE BASIL:** The kind often used in Italian cooking. Works well muddled into all sorts of drinks, cooked into syrups, and infused into spirits such as vodka or gin.

○ **GARDEN THYME:** Most commonly used in cooking, and great in syrups.

○ **LEMON THYME:** A lemony-flavored thyme variation for both cooking and syrups.

○ **CORIANDER:** Also called cilantro or Chinese parsley, has a fresh distinctive taste.

○ **LEMON VERBENA:** Superb for tea, syrups, smashes.

○ **SAGE:** Also called salvia, sage grows wild in many parts of the world, such as the Southwestern United States, where it is often used in cooking, and imparts a lovely earthy quality. Look for flavorful variations of this plant such as pineapple sage for your edible cocktail experiments.

○ **LAVENDER:** Although lavender could go into the flower section of this chapter, its application is more like that of an herb, and it is, in essence, an herb plant. English lavender is most used in cooking, and therefore ideal for cocktails, but feel free to experiment if you find other varieties in your neck of the proverbial woods.

- **GINGER:** This root is ideal for cocktails. Its zing makes for a spicy element when muddled into a cocktail glass, boiled to make a syrup, or candied to be used as a garnish.

- **THAI CHILIS:** These are ideal for infusing into oils, spirits, and syrups.

- **WORMWOOD:** Try growing a wormwood bush if you are feeling really adventurous and want to infuse the bark into a clear spirit, such as vodka. Wormwood is the main ingredient in absinthe, an anise-tasting liqueur, which has a lot of history, lore, and myth surrounding its supposed psychedelic qualities (which, by the way, are largely untrue). These bushes do particularly well in more arid climates.

DRINK YOUR VEGGIES

Your family doctor or nutritionist will recommend that you have at least five servings of fruits and vegetables per day. Who says they can't come by way of a martini glass? In fact, you will probably be surprised at how many vegetables you can take from garden to glass! This is a suggestion list, but why not see how far you can go with veggies that you'd never before considered as cocktail ingredients?

○ **CHERRY TOMATOES:** Great for garnishes and muddling.

○ **GREEN TOMATOES:** A crisp, almost apple-like quality, interesting for jams.

○ **YELLOW TOMATOES:** A slightly sweeter, fun variation for Tomato Water (see recipe in Chapter 6) and garnishes.

- **HEIRLOOM TOMATOES:** The commercial, almost-tasteless, homogenous tomatoes that you buy in supermarkets are hybrid varietals that grow quickly and produce a quick profit for large-scale farmers. Heirloom tomatoes, on the other hand, come from seeds that have remained relatively pure over decades, and are passed down within families or farming communities (hence the term "heirloom"). The more natural heirloom tomatoes come in varying colors, shapes, and sizes, as opposed to the uniform tomatoes you are likely used to seeing at chain stores, so bring a bit of healthful variety to your juices and cocktails by using the more diverse heirloom tomatoes.

- **CUCUMBERS:** Great muddled, sliced for garnishes, or juiced for fresh summertime drinks. Experiment with different varieties of cucumbers to use in drinks, and even consider pickling some to use as garnishes for libations such as the Bloody Mary.

- **CARROTS:** An interesting—and healthy—ingredient for alcoholic and nonalcoholic cocktails. It is packed with vitamins and flavor, mixes well with other juices (such as apple, orange, or beet), and also plays nicely in the glass with spirits such as vodka and gin.

- **BEETS:** Naturally sweet, incredibly healthful, and full of iron, beet juice has an earthy quality and pairs well with spirits such as gin and vodka.

- **BELL PEPPERS:** Red and yellow bell peppers are particularly tasty in muddled drinks as they have a slightly sweeter taste than green bell peppers, which make for interesting garnishes.

- **JALAPEÑO PEPPERS:** A multifaceted ingredient; muddle some jalapeño into a spicy margarita, cook it into a syrup or jam, or infuse it directly into a spirit to bring some heat to your drinks.

- **GREEN AND RED CHILIES:** Abundant in the Southwestern United States, these chilies can be muddled directly into drinks (like the other peppers mentioned in this section). They can also be bought in powdered form and infused or cooked into syrups, oils, and spirits.

- **RHUBARB:** Most thought of as being used in pies and other baked goodies, but is amazing for syrups and jams used in cocktails (see Rhubarb and Fennel Syrup recipe in Chapter 4).

- **PUMPKIN:** Cook, purée, and use for thick, delicious, dessert-style holiday cocktails (see Pumpkin Purée recipe in Chapter 4).

- **ACORN SQUASH:** May not spring to mind when thinking about cocktails but when cooked and puréed, is an interesting ingredient, particularly for winter time holidays (such as Thanksgiving in the United States) when squash is in season.

GET FRUITY

Fruits are a no-brainer when it comes to cocktails. In fact, any kind of fruit can find its way into a cocktail glass and be a welcome addition. Depending on where you live and how much growing area is available to you, you can go as nuts as you like with all kinds of fruit!

○ **BERRIES:** Blackberries, raspberries, gooseberries, and blueberries are wonderful muddled into various versions of a mojito or margarita, for example, but berries also lend themselves beautifully to jams, syrups, and purées. Double strain the cocktails when muddling berries directly into the cocktail shaker because they are apt to leave behind seeds or little floating bits of fruit flesh that don't belong in a cocktail.

○ **STONE FRUITS:** Cherries, peaches, and apricots are not only great muddled directly into a cocktail shaker but also cooked into jams, syrups, and purées. They are also ideal for homemade fruit-infused brandies and liqueurs.

○ **HARVEST FRUITS:** Apples, pears, and avocados ripen in the autumn (in the Northern Hemisphere). Freshly pressed juices and ciders have all sorts of applications for both

cooking and fall-inspired cocktails. Also consider experimenting with things like muddled avocado in a cocktail (gives a silky texture, see The Guayabera in Chapter 7), or home-made apple butter (as used in the Harvest Hot-Buttered Rum in Chapter 5).

- ○ **CITRUS FRUITS:** An absolute must if your environment is conducive to growing them. Lemon, Meyer (sweet) lemon, lime, orange, grapefruit, and kumquats are all wonderful squeezed into cocktails as well as made into marmalades and syrups. These are also ideal for making candied citrus garnishes, as seen in Chapter 6.

- ○ **LYCHEES:** These small, round, subtly flavored Asian fruits are especially wonderful in sake- and vodka-based cocktails. If you don't have the climate to grow them, look for canned ones in Asian or gourmet supermarkets.

- ○ **TROPICAL FRUITS:** Persimmon, mango, pineapple, and coconut are amazing in all sorts of cocktails beyond the rum-based drinks with which we are mostly familiar. Try them with whiskey or tequila.

EDIBLE FLOWERS

Humans have been using flowers as symbols of love, and for personal beautification, religious offerings, and medicinal purposes throughout history. It is no wonder that flowers have also found their way into our diets. In fact, whether eating stuffed squash blossoms or drinking jasmine tea, you include flowers as a bigger part of your diet than you may realize. Creative chefs incorporate edible flowers into dishes from salads to savory fare in fine restaurants. It's even commonplace to find packages of organic edible flowers in high-end grocery stores. Of course, the bartenders and mixologists have not overlooked edible flowers either.

Distillation of herbal and floral infusions began as an ancient medical practice and for centuries, flowers have been, and continue to be, brewed into natural remedies in homeopathic health treatments. As those skills and techniques spread around the globe, some cultures began using that knowledge to create what we know today as spirits. As with all forms of distilled

alcoholic concoctions used for health or pleasure, these spirits often needed sugar to make them more palatable. This sugar inclusion was the birth of both cocktails and liqueurs. As a matter of fact, herbal- and floral-infused spirits and liqueurs are making a huge comeback in modern mixology; today flowers such as violet, elderflower, jasmine, lavender, hibiscus, and rose are showing up as options in liqueurs and syrups. And, of course, garnishes, orange flower water, and rose water are often used in cocktails, too.

Edible flowers are a creative element of the edible cocktail. The blooms can be cooked into a homemade ingredient. They can also be frozen into the water in your ice cube tray to make gorgeous ice cubes for your cocktails. And, flowers can be floated on the surface of a drink to bring a unique appearance to a distinctive cocktail. A variety of edible flowers are available at farmers' markets and grocery chains (such as Whole Foods) for food and drink garnishes and some are easy to find or grow yourself. Consider the following:

- **CHAMOMILE:** This flower is known for its calming properties. It is most often dried and used in teas aimed at soothing a sour stomach or helping a person sleep. Chamomile tea can be used in cocktails and punches, and it can also be cooked with equal parts sugar to make a chamomile syrup to use in drinks.

- **HIBISCUS:** Sometimes also called *flor de Jamaica*, hibiscus petals can be steeped in hot water to make a tea. That tea can be used directly in drinks or cooked into a syrup. Hibiscus juice is also beginning to appear on grocery store shelves, and is a fun ingredient for creative cocktails.

- **ELDERFLOWER:** This small white flower typically grows on the hillsides of southern France. Romantic lore says that these flowers only bloom for a few weeks per year, so the fragile blossoms must be hand collected during that specific time. The elderflowers have a wonderful fragrance and are often cooked into syrups to preserve the aroma and flavor long after the flowers have died. There are also elderflower-infused spirits and liqueurs available in stores.

- **JASMINE:** The delicate fragrance of the jasmine flower makes it attractive to mixologists wanting to bring a softness and subtlety to a creative cocktail. Also commonly used in teas, jasmine can be cooked into homemade cocktail ingredients as well as infused into spirits and liqueurs.

- **GINGER FLOWERS:** The flowers that spring out of the earth are nearly as versatile as the more commonly used ginger root growing beneath it. They can be incorporated into teas and syrups and used as decorative garnishes.

○ **ANGELICA:** This blossom has a unique celery flavor so it brings an unusual element to food and cocktails.

○ **BEGONIA:** The blooms of begonia have a sour, citrusy taste.

○ **BORAGE:** This plant is also known as the starflower. It has a cucumber flavor.

○ **CALENDULA:** Calendula (also known as pot marigold) can be a bit bitter with a hint of spiciness.

○ **CITRUS BLOSSOMS:** The blossoms of plants such as lemon, lime, and orange are lovely, fragrant garnishes. Orange blossom–infused water is often used in old-time cocktails as well as in Mediterranean cooking. It is found ready-made in gourmet or ethnic food shops as well as many high-end liquor stores.

○ **DANDELIONS:** These flowers have an "umami" or savory quality and can be a fascinating ingredient when cooked into syrups, for example. However, be sure to only buy dandelions raised for culinary purposes, or perhaps ones in the wild. Be wary of any dandelions in parks or in peoples' yards as they are considered weeds and therefore may have been sprayed with weed-killing chemicals.

○ **DAY LILIES:** These are one of the only edible types of lilies. They have a crisp texture.

○ **FENNEL FLOWERS:** The blooms of fennel have a fresh, licorice flavor.

○ **VIOLET:** This flower has a sweet flavor and is often used in candies, syrups, and liqueurs.

The Pimm's Secret

According to mixologist and consultant Nick Strangeway, the Pimm's No. 1 (used in the classic Pimm's Cup Cocktail) first launched with a packet of borage flowers as garnish. Although the recipe for Pimm's No. 1 is a closely guarded secret, that may be a little clue as to one of the important ingredients.

53

Farmers' Market

If you're not able to grow your own cocktail garden, don't worry, you can find the majority of the herbs, vegetables, fruits, and flowers at your local farmers' market. No matter where you live, there are farmers' markets in every major metropolitan area, and the majority of them are held at least once or twice per week. Wandering from stall to stall, choosing cheese, produce, juices, flowers, and so on from the people who often grew or made these items themselves, brings a feeling of small-town community even if you're living in a big city. And, as you delve further into the idea of market-fresh mixology, a weekend stroll through your local market will come alive with new possibilities for you.

You may already be accustomed to looking at the farmers' market as a great place to fill your refrigerator, so ideally, this book will inspire you to look at it also as a great source to stock your bar. Of course, the stands selling fresh herbs and fruit are the obvious first stops when thinking about cocktails. In many farmers' markets you'll find fresh mint for mojitos, limes for margaritas, and seasonal berries to muddle and shake into delicious fruity cocktails. However, thinking beyond the obvious will bring new excitement to your cocktail shaker and martini glass. For example, honey, lavender, farm-fresh eggs, and spicy chilies are also intriguing elements to bring into your mixology. Here are a few tips to making the most of your farmers' market offerings.

BECOME A REGULAR

Find the most convenient market for you, and go there on a regular basis. Get to know the vendors and form friendly relationships with them. Let the local producers know that you are interested in whatever is coming up in seasonal produce, and ask them to put some aside for you. Not only is this relationship mutually beneficial businesswise—meaning that you will have the inside track to the best of seasonal ingredients—but you also may wind up with a new friend who holds similar culinary interests!

ASK QUESTIONS

The people selling at these kinds of local markets are often the same people who grow, make, or produce the items they bring there. Ask them about the ingredients: How do *they*, the growers, use them? How are the items made or grown? Does the vendor have food or drink recipes to share? What kind of other ingredients partner well with some of the specific items you are buying? Inspiration is everywhere, and even if someone doesn't practice mixology, their use of seasonal ingredients could spark an idea for your next creation.

Nurture Nature

Growing your own herbs, fruits, veggies, and flowers to use in your own cooking and cocktail making is such a satisfying experience; here's hoping you decide to nurture at least a pot of commonly used herbs to keep on your kitchen countertop. But whether or not gardening becomes a passionate pastime for you, this chapter should have made you realize that fresh ingredients make great drinks. Growing, gathering, and hunting for these ingredients can be a big part of the fun. And now it's time to take this knowledge to the next level, and learn how you can use these fresh finds in both your kitchen and your bar.

CHAPTER 3

Grape to Glass

CULTURALLY, WINE IS MORE THAN FERMENTED
GRAPE JUICE. IT REPRESENTS MANY THINGS IN
MANY COUNTRIES. FOR SOME, WINE MAY REPRESENT ROMANCE
and dinners for two. For others, wine expresses characteristics of a specific
grape, climate, or region. For example, drinking a malbec from Argentina or
champagne from France is a way not only to punctuate a night with friends
or unwind at the end of the day, but also to take a sip of a place that you may
love or dream of visiting someday. In addition, each winemaker, or vintner,
leaves his or her unique fingerprint upon the wine he or she creates. From
choosing the moment to harvest the grapes, to deciding how long the wine
should ferment or age in wood, and finally determining which vintages should
be blended with one another, the winemaker uses a combination of technical
skill and gut instinct. In a sense, it's not so different from creating a cocktail.

When you open a bottle of wine, you are sipping a finished product. The
winemaker has put time, thought, and care into growing, fermenting, and
blending his or her grapes into the elixir you pour into your glass. However,
nice wine, like a fine spirit, can be a wonderful base for an inspired cocktail.
In fact, while most people may think of wine and cocktails as being an either/
or choice, wine and fortified wine enhance many a classic cocktail. Take the

martini, for example. Early recipes for that drink called for gin and dry vermouth with an optional dash of bitters. Vermouth's inclusion offered a much richer and more complex-tasting drink than the modern "two shots of chilled vodka with an olive" version served more widely in bars and restaurants today. In addition, refreshing, fruity sangria (wine-based punch) has long been served in sunny Spain—and it's a great way to use young or inexpensive wine that may still be a little rough around the edges. However, high-end mixology also incorporates wine, fortified wine, and of course, grape-based spirits.

This chapter is meant to take some of the mystery out of wine, sparkling wine, fortified wines—such as vermouth, sherry, and port—as well as grape-based spirits such as brandy. Here you'll learn what makes a great wine and what the different kinds of wine can bring to your cocktail. And you'll find some recipes for creative cocktails that include a variety of red, white, sparkling, and fortified wines. Before you know it, you'll be popping a cork and pulling out the cocktail shaker!

What's in Your Wine?

Grapes remain one of the largest and heartiest crops on earth. They grow on most continents and thrive in somewhat arid regions boasting warm summers and relatively mild winters. From countries whose shores are lapped by the Mediterranean Sea to the rolling hills of northern California, to the wild yet sophisticated Hunter Valley in Australia to majestic mountainous regions of South America, grapevines flourish in some of the most beautiful spots on the globe.

Off the Vine

Grapevines do particularly well on sandy or clay-rich soils. They like lots of sun and are often planted on sunny slopes. The vines should be pruned (and sometimes covered) in the winter months. In the spring and summer, the plants will start to bloom and grow again. The grapes are harvested in the autumn and pressed to extract the juice, which is then fermented. While some wines are meant to be consumed when "young" (not aged) most wine is aged in wood barrels for some amount of time.

But not all grapes are equal and not all grapes are appropriate for winemaking. Here you'll learn about what grapes you'll find in the most popular wines and what you can expect from each of these wines.

WHITE WINES

White grapes range from very light in color (almost whitish) to more of a greenish hue. Sometimes the grapes even have a hint of honey color to them. The juice inside is clear, and the skins leave very little color in the wines the grapes create. In fact, when a white wine has a golden color in the glass, it is often acquired from the wooden casks in which the wine may have been aged. The following wines are made from these sweet, white grapes:

○ **CHARDONNAY:** This wine is made from one of the most widely grown grapes, and it is grown worldwide because of its ability to flourish in a variety of soils. It has a somewhat fruity aroma and is often known for a "buttery" finish, particularly when aged in oak.

○ **RIESLING:** The Riesling grapes that make up this wine grow well in cooler regions. A common misconception is that Riesling is a sweet wine but in fact it can actually be quite delightfully dry.

○ **SAUVIGNON BLANC:** This light, herbaceous wine has higher levels of acidity than other wines, which make this variety of wine delicious when paired with food or when sipped on its own. The Sauvignon Blanc grape grows worldwide but some particularly popular brands of wine made from this grape come from New Zealand.

○ **PINOT GRIS / PINOT GRIGIO:** The grape used to make this wine tends to grow in cooler climates. It is a light wine with lower acidity.

○ **VIOGNIER:** This wine hails primarily from the Rhone region of France. It is showing up on more wine lists worldwide as its lovely floral aroma makes wine lovers swoon.

The Apéro

An apéritif is an appetite opener, and most often consists of a forti-fied wine (vermouth or sherry, for example) or a glass of bubbly. It is not uncommon to serve a sparkling cocktail, either, such as a Kir Royale (cassis liqueur and champagne). In France, for example, sharing a before-dinner tipple with friends is so common that the event has its own slang term, the apéro.

RED WINES

Red grapes can range in color from pinkish to deep purple. The juice inside the fruit, however, is clear. Red wine gets its color from resting with the skins, which impart their hue upon the resulting juice. Some color is also acquired from the wood. Typically, the darker the grape, the richer the wine. The following wines are made from these red grapes:

○ **PINOT NOIR:** This grape makes for a soft, pleasant, lighter red wine and a good starting point for the "red wine–curious." Its balance allows it to be enjoyed with light fare such as poultry and even fish, as opposed to many other red wines, which are considered solely red meat–friendly.

○ **MERLOT:** Merlot grapes also make for a lighter red wine, whose popularity has risen and fallen over the years according to the whims of pop culture. For example, when one of the characters in the film *Sideways* declared a strong preference for pinot noir over merlot, U.S. sales fell notably. However, merlot is once again on the rise as it is a wonderful varietal that can be enjoyed with lighter fare.

○ **CABERNET SAUVIGNON:** Cabernet Sauvignon is perhaps the most widely grown red wine grape. The resulting wine has full body and flavor, making it both food-friendly and a robust sip on its own.

○ **GRENACHE:** Grenache grapes grow in much of the world, but particularly like hot, dry climates. They do very well in Spain and southern France, for example. Grenache wine is bold and spicy and its berry notes make it a good candidate for blending with other grape varietals, resulting in delicious blended red wines.

○ **SYRAH / SHIRAZ:** Syrah grapes come from the Mediterranean region as well as northern California. The grapes are also grown in Australia where they are called Shiraz. This dark red wine has bold flavor and high tannin, making it a wine that can be paired with spicy food and bold wine-based cocktails.

○ **LAMBRUSCO:** An Italian red grape that is used in both flat and sparkling lambrusco red wine. It is relatively dry and when made into a sparkling wine, it is quite fizzy with small, streaming bubbles, and usually referred to as a *frizzante*.

○ **RED ZINFANDEL:** Red zinfandel grapes are often associated with northern California. Their wine is big, bold, spicy, and robust. It pairs well with wild game and plays nicely with fresh berries and red fruits in cocktails.

SPARKLING WINES

Sparkling wine is made throughout the world, and the name by which it goes varies according to the region in which it is produced. Carbonation can be added several ways but the most famous, perhaps, is *méthode champenoise*, which is the traditional way of making sparkling wine in Champagne, France. In this method, the bubbles come from in-bottle fermentation. However, other producers make the wine first and add carbonation later. Below are a few terms for sparkling wine from various parts of the world:

○ **CHAMPAGNE:** It is law that only sparkling wine from the Champagne region of France can be called "champagne." While other wine makers may use the same grapes, methods of production, and blending techniques, no other wine producer outside this region can call their product by this name.

○ **CAVA:** Sparkling wine from Spain is referred to as *cava.* It is made in a few regions around the country including northern Spain, or Catalonia. Many higher-end cava producers also employ the méthode champenoise.

○ **PROSECCO:** This is the name of both the wine and the grape used to make this Italian sparkling wine. It is light and fruity—a great summer sipper—and typically not made via méthode champenoise.

○ **SPARKLING WINE:** This is the general term for bubbly made in other parts of the world. Sparkling wines can be on the sweet and fruity side, or they can be less sweet (brut) or quite dry (extra brut).

FORTIFIED WINE

When a wine is referred to as "fortified," it means that some distilled spirit (usually brandy, a grape-based spirit) has been added to it both for preservation and flavor. As with sparkling wines, the name of the wine is often associated with its region of origin, such as:

○ **MADEIRA:** A fortified wine made on the Portuguese island of the same name.

○ **MARSALA:** An Italian version of fortified wine that is made specifically on the island of Sicily. Frequently used in cooking (as in Chicken Marsala), this fortified wine can also be used in cocktails.

○ **PORT:** This wine gets its name from the picturesque seaside town of Porto in Portugal, and the grapes are mainly grown in the Douro Valley. Although it can be enjoyed as an apéritif, or incorporated into food-friendly cocktails, it is most often thought of as an after-dinner drink. As with wine, it can be aged in the bottle or in a wooden barrel. Two of the most common types of port are ruby, which is bright red and generally drunk relatively young; and tawny, which gets more of a brownish color and richer, nutty flavor from being aged in wood.

○ **SHERRY:** This wine is like champagne in that it is protected by a designation of origin. Only fortified wine from within the "sherry triangle" in the southern part of Spain can be called sherry. It is often aged in a solera system in which barrels are stacked upon one another in a sort of pyramid, and some of the older sherries get blended into the younger barrels, making for a richer end result.

○ **VERMOUTH:** Vermouth is a fortified wine infused with herbs and spices, which originally got its name from the German word for wormwood—even though wormwood is actually integral to absinthe (an anise-flavored, herbal liqueur) and is not found in all vermouths. Vermouth is probably the most recognizable fortified wine used in cocktails. As dry vermouth (almost clear in color), it is integral to the classic martini, and sweet vermouth (which is a bit sweeter and red in color) remains a main ingredient in the manhattan. Vermouth is also delicious on its own, and often served that way in Europe as an apéritif.

○ **ICE WINE / EISWEIN:** This is a sweet wine made from grapes that have been frozen on the grapevine, resulting in a naturally concentrated sweetness and flavor. It is usually served as a dessert wine and is also a lovely moderator in cocktails. Due to climate, ice wine is particularly common in Germany (and other parts of northern Europe) as well as Canada.

○ **LILLET:** This wine is a brand of French apéritif wine. It is made from Bordeaux grapes blended with citrus liqueurs (primarily bitter orange and grapefruit). Like vermouth, it comes in both red and white. It is delicious on its own, chilled or over ice, and it is also a wonderful ingredient in an aromatic, elegant cocktail.

Digesting a Digestif

A digestif is an after-dinner drink meant to help the body digest a meal. These drinks can be liqueurs infused with herbs thought to aid digestion or often they are a grape-based spirit, such as cognac or Armagnac, or a rich fortified wine such as port. All can also be incorporated into cocktails and served with or without food.

Grape-Based Spirits

As we discussed in Chapter 1, many spirits, such as whiskey, are grain based. The initial fermentation of those grains results in a beer. When that beer is distilled, it becomes a high-proof alcohol that is usually aged for some amount of time in wood casks, and then blended with water to bring down the percentage of alcohol enough so that the product is fit for human consumption. The process for grape-based spirits is pretty much the same: Grape-based spirits begin as wine. The grape juice is fermented, and then it is put through the distillation process. Most wines range from 12 to 15 percent alcohol by volume. Once distilled however, they become a clear, high-proof spirit that is aged and brought down to about 40 percent alcohol (eighty proof). Here's a list of the most commonly used grape-based spirits:

○ **GRAPE-BASED VODKA:** The most simple distilled wine is grape-based vodka, such as Cïroc and Grey Goose, both made in French wine-making regions.

○ **BRANDY:** Brandy is the most common grape-based spirit and is made from wine grapes in the wine-growing regions of France (such as Cognac and Armagnac), Spain (such as Brandy de Jerez), and South America (such as pisco, originally distilled from wine sur- plus in Chile and Peru). The word "brandy" comes from the Dutch word *brandewijn*, which literally means burnt wine. Brandy, wherever it is made, begins as wine that is then distilled. The region and method by which it is produced defines the name by which it is called:

> **Cognac, Armagnac:** This spirit is mainly made from the fermented juices of uni blanc, folle blanche, and Colombard grapes in the Cognac, and smaller Armagnac, regions which are nestled just north of the famed wine-growing region of Bordeaux, France.

> **Brandy de Jerez:** Although the grapes used to make Spanish brandy come from other regions around Spain, Brandy de Jerez is produced in the Jerez de la Frontera region in the southern part of the country from Spanish sherry. One of the things that makes Spanish brandy unique is its aging system called solera (as described in the sherry description above) in which liquid is taken from older barrels and mixed into younger ones, thereby making for richer, more flavorful end products.

> **Brandy de Penedes:** Brandy de Penedes is a lesser-known Catalan brandy made in the wine-growing region of Penedes, near the French border. In these brandies, both French and Spanish grapes can be used.

Pisco: Pisco is sometimes referred to as South American brandy. It is made specifically in Chile and Peru. It has a long and interesting history, which begins with Spanish priests bringing grapes to South America to make wine for Mass. The grapes flourished to such an extent in these areas that the monks and priests began to distill their overabundance of wine into a clear spirit. Although the town of Pisco is in Peru, to this day, Chile and Peru continue a friendly battle over which country has the right to call pisco its own.

Grappa: Grappa is a sort of cross between brandy and vodka but it's a bit rougher than the usual because it is made from the leftover pomace (left over stems, seeds, and grape skins) rather than the purer, smoother grape juice. Grappa is drunk on its own but can be more pleasant in cocktails because the other ingredients soften its flavor.

○ **OUZO:** Ouzo is a brandy from Greece that is made from pressed grapes and infused with herbs and botanicals. It is most often drunk on its own after a meal as a digestif.

○ **G'VINE:** G'Vine is a brand of grape-based gin. It is unique among gins because most are made from grain-based spirits. G'Vine is made in Cognac, from the same uni blanc grapes used in both wine and cognac brandy. In order to be labeled gin, however, the spirit must be infused with juniper, which G'Vine is, as well as with several other flowers and botanicals from the Cognac region. If you are looking for an interesting variation on gin, and want to explore grape-based spirits, this could be a good one to try.

Grape-Based Cocktails

Using wine and grape-based spirits has been part of mixology ever since people began mixing alcohol. The recipes below include a few classics that every cocktail-lover should know, as well as new drinks from modern tastemakers behind bars around the world. If you are going to pair these cocktails with food, you'll want to follow classic-style cocktail recipes, which are not too sweet, and mainly consist of spirits. A classic sparkling cocktail will often go well with a light first course; an aromatic spirit (such as gin) or a dark spirit (such as bourbon) used as a cocktail base can bring out layers of flavor in a main meat dish; and a luscious ruby port-based cocktail will make a chocolate torte soar.

{ Pisco Sour }

½ ounce lemon or lime juice (can also be half lemon and half lime juice)

½ ounce Basic Simple Syrup (Chapter 4) *or* 1 heaping tablespoon powdered sugar

1½ ounces pisco

½ egg white (see more about using eggs in cocktails in Chapter 5)

Dash Angostura bitters

This classic drink is important to have in your bartending repertoire. It is light and refreshing, and a hallmark South American cocktail. Pisco is made in both Peru and Chile and each country lays claim to it as its national cocktail. There are many slight variations on the recipe, so you'll see a few options in the directions, below.

· · · · ·

1. Combine the lemon juice, Basic Simple Syrup, pisco, and egg white in a cocktail shaker. Give the mix a strenuous "dry shake" (no ice) to get the egg white nice and frothy.

2. Then, reopen the cocktail shaker and add ice. Shake vigorously again. Strain into a chilled martini or cocktail glass.

3. Garnish with a few drops of Angostura bitters floating on the foamy surface of the drink. (This is sometimes served in a champagne flute or in a rocks glass over ice.)

{ Southern Sage }

1 sprig sage

½ ounce Smoked-Sage Syrup
(Chapter 4)

½ ounce fresh grapefruit
juice

½ ounce Limoncello Della
Casa (Chapter 5)

1½ ounces pisco

Dash orange bitters

This aromatic cocktail mingles fresh sage with sweet lemon and tangy grapefruit, balancing nicely with a grape-based pisco. The aroma and layered flavors create a fully well-rounded experience for the senses.

. . . . .

Pluck a couple of sage leaves from the sprig, and muddle them with the Smoked-Sage Syrup in the bottom of a mixing glass. Add remaining liquid ingredients. Shake vigorously with ice. Double strain into a martini glass or into an ice-filled rocks glass. Garnish with remainder of sage sprig and bitters.

{ Classic Martini }

½ ounce vermouth

2 ounces gin
(vodka may be substituted
for a vodka martini)

¼ ounce olive juice
(if you want a "dirty" martini)

GARNISH: a couple of stuffed
olives, a lemon twist, or a
cocktail onion is the most
common garnish.

Originally, a martini was made from just about equal parts gin and vermouth (sweet vermouth was even commonly used). Today, hard-core mixologists going toward a classic martini will use 2 parts gin to 1 part dry vermouth. This recipe dials back the vermouth a little bit more though as most people are not accustomed to drinking vermouth-heavy martinis.

· · · · ·

Pour all liquid ingredients into a mixing glass. Fill with ice. Stir the drink with a long bar spoon for at least 30 seconds. Use the julep strainer to strain the drink into a chilled martini glass. Add the garnish.

Garnishes on Ice

Keeping your garnishes cool is a great tip for a great drink. Think about it—why plop warm, room-temperature cherries, olives, cocktail onions, etc., into a drink you've just chilled with ice? Keep the drink and the garnish cold by storing them in the refrigerator or on ice.

{ Burnt-Cherry Manhattan }

GARNISH: flamed marinated cherry

¾ ounce sweet vermouth

2 ounces whiskey (can be rye or bourbon)

Dash bitters (Angostura is the go-to bitters, but feel free to use flavored bitters sometimes for a creative twist)

Manhattan lovers can be quite particular about how they like their drink pre- pared. Again, when it was first created this drink was heavy on the sweet ver- mouth (almost equal parts in the early days), but today has several variations. A dry martini calls for dry vermouth instead of sweet. A "perfect" martini uses equal parts sweet and dry vermouth. This recipe is based on a pretty classic Manhattan recipe with a bit of fiery flair from the flamed marinated cherry.

• • • • •

1. Flame a marinated cherry by placing it in a martini glass and spraying it with flaming rum mixture as described in Chapter 6 and lighting it on fire. Let it burn for a few seconds. When flame goes out, set aside glass.

2. Pour all remaining ingredients into a mixing glass. Fill with ice. Stir for at least 30 seconds until chilled. Use the julep strainer to strain into a chilled martini glass. Drop cherry into the drink as garnish.

{ Sidecar }

½ ounce fresh lemon juice

¾ ounce orange liqueur
(Cointreau, for example)

2 ounces cognac

GARNISH: sugar rim

The historic Sidecar cocktail was created during Prohibition in the 1920s. It is a great example of a cognac- or brandy-based cocktail and is a delicious introduction to grape-based classic drinks.

. . . . .

Rim a martini glass with sugar, set aside. Pour all ingredients into a cocktail shaker. Fill with ice, shake vigorously. Strain into sugar-rimmed glass.

{ G'Vine Hanky Panky }

GARNISH: flamed orange round

1½ ounces G'Vine Nouaison grape-based gin

1½ ounces sweet vermouth

2 dashes Fernet Branca

The original Hanky Panky cocktail recipe was created at the American Bar at the Savoy Hotel in London, in 1925. This recipe stays very close to the original in proportions and concept, but instead of the usual grain-based gin and vermouth, calls for the grape-based G'Vine gin instead.

. . . . .

Flame an orange round, as described in the garnish section of this book, over a chilled martini glass (directions in Chapter 6). Set aside. Pour all ingredients into a mixing glass. Fill with ice, and stir for at least 30 seconds. Strain into glass.

{ Flaming Angelico }

Spritz flaming orange bitters

¼ ounce maraschino liqueur

¾ ounce Hibiscus-Cabernet Syrup (Chapter 4)

¾ ounce lemon juice

2 ounces Gran Centenario Rosangel Hibiscus-Infused Tequila

GARNISH: lemon twirl

Wine can be used as a direct ingredient in cocktails, and also as a base for syrups. The cabernet syrup found in this recipe plays off of the hibiscus notes in the Gran Centenario hibiscus-infused tequila. The richness wine brings to this syrup stands up to the power of the tequila, and is another great example of how to use wine in mixology.

· · · · ·

Flame a martini glass by spritzing it with the flaming orange bitters mixture and lighting it on fire (explained in Chapter 6). Pour all liquid ingredients into a cocktail shaker. Add ice and shake well. Strain into the flamed glass. Garnish with lemon twirl draped over the side of the glass.

{ Skid Rosa }

1 strawberry (medium sized)

4 cucumber slices

1 ounce Il Conte d'Alba Stella Rosa Rosso

½ ounce Ketel One Citron Vodka

1½ ounces Homemade Sweet and Sour Mix (Chapter 6)

Stella Rosa Rosso—a delicious, lightly sweet, and fruity, sparkling red wine is made from Italian Brachetto grapes, and lends itself to being enjoyed with cheeses on its own, or as the base ingredient for this farmers' market–fresh cocktail.

· · · · ·

Muddle strawberry and 3 cucumber slices. Add the rest of the liquid ingredients. Shake well with ice. Strain into an ice-filled collins glass. Garnish with the remaining cucumber slice sitting on the rim of the glass or tucked just inside the top of the glass, in the drink.

{ Tuscan Refresher }

6 large sweet basil leaves

1 ounce homemade Lemon-Lime Syrup (Chapter 4)

¼ ounce Square One Basil Vodka

2 ounces Grappa Moscato

¼ ounce Strega liqueur (an Italian herbal liqueur)

GARNISH: Candied Limes (Chapter 6)

This grappa-based cocktail is balanced with fresh sweet homemade lime syrup and an Italian herbal liqueur. Grappa is not commonly used in cocktails, so this drink is something a bit out of the ordinary and is a great way to incorporate a less-commonly used spirit in a unique mixed drink.

• • • • •

Muddle the basil, syrup, and basil vodka in a cocktail shaker. Add the grappa and ice and shake vigorously. Strain into an ice-filled collins glass. Drizzle ¼ ounce of Strega liqueur over the top. Garnish with a Candied Lime Wheel.

¾ ounce Tanqueray gin

¾ ounce Campari

¾ ounce Italian sweet vermouth

¾ ounce Shiraz wine

½ ounce Licor 43

2 dashes Fee Brothers Old Fashion Bitters

GARNISH: Candied Orange (Chapter 6)

The classic Negroni cocktail was created in Florence, Italy, in the early 1900s in honor of Count Camilo Negroni (an Italian aristocrat known to frequent local cocktail bars). The original recipe calls for equal parts gin, Campari (an Italian bitter liqueur), and sweet vermouth. This recipe puts a twist on the classic by incorporating Shiraz, a popular wine grape grown "down under."

· · · · ·

Stir ingredients, except for garnish, with ice in a mixing glass. Strain into an ice-filled wine glass or chilled cocktail glass. Add garnish.

{ Spring Sherry Cobbler }

⅓ ounce fresh lemon juice

⅓ ounce Pineapple Syrup
(Chapter 4)

1 ounce PX Sherry

1 ounce Lillet Blanc

5 dashes Dr. Elmegirab's
Dandelion & Burdock Bitters

GARNISH: sprig each of fresh
thyme and mint, and a lemon
wheel

Sherry and Lillet Blanc are both grape-based but they bring varying qualities to the cocktail. The slightly sweet, aged PX sherry balances nicely against the drier, white Lillet, making for a unique cocktail-sipping experience.

· · · · ·

Place all ingredients except garnish materials into a glass filled with crushed ice, stir briskly. This will melt some of the crushed ice, so "crown" the glass with more. Garnish with the thyme, mint, and lemon.

{ Aloe Pompier }

1 ounce Massenez Crème de
Cassis de Dijon

1 ounce Noilly Prat French
dry vermouth

¼ ounce fresh lemon juice

Aloe vera soda (or club soda)

GARNISH: lemon wedge, mint
sprig, and cherry

This cocktail is a simple twist on a lovely French classic cocktail the "Pompier," made up of dry vermouth, crème de cassis, and club soda. The big amount of sweetness brought by the cassis is perfectly balanced by the vermouth. If you can find aloe vera soda, it gives a unique flavor. If that is not available, club soda will work too.

· · · · ·

Pour first four ingredients into a cocktail shaker. Shake with ice. Strain into a collins glass. Garnish with a lemon wedge, mint sprig, and cherry.

{ The Duchess }

2 ounces Lillet Blanc

½ ounce Licor 43

½ ounce fresh-squeezed
lemon juice

2 ounces Fever-Tree or Q
Tonic water

GARNISH: 3 Quick-Pickled
Grapes (Chapter 6)

The Duchess of Windsor, a controversial socialite and tastemaker who never travelled without a case of Lillet in her luggage, was the inspiration for this drink. The story goes that if the duchess ran out of Lillet at a party in southern France, a case had to be immediately shipped down from Paris, because no other apéritif would do the trick.

· · · · ·

Pour all liquid ingredients over ice in a collins (tall) glass, stir to chill and incorporate. Garnish with 3 quick-pickled grapes on a skewer.

{ Ice Wine Martini }

1½ ounces vodka

¾ ounce ice wine

Dash Fee Brothers Grapefruit
Bitters

Eiswein or ice wine, with its intense aroma, sweetness, and smooth finish, is punched up to the next level when mixed with an ice-cold vodka. This drink is at its best when served as a classic martini-style apéritif.

· · · · ·

Pour all ingredients into a mixing glass. Fill with ice and stir well. Strain into a chilled martini glass.

Sparkling Cocktails

The pop of a cork punctuates a celebration like no other sound can. Guests can't help but comment and smile when they hear it. It's funny to think that a bit of fermented grape juice can make such an impact—but it does! Using sparkling wine in cocktails brings an extra element of fun and festivity to any gathering, so here are a few suggestions for your next celebration.

{ Classic Champagne Cocktail }

1 sugar cube

3 dashes Angostura bitters

4 ounces sparkling wine

The classic champagne cocktail is simple, classy, and impresses guests more than just a glass of sparkling wine because of the extra oomph a dash of bitters imparts. Plus the extra step in preparation makes guests feel like they are getting the "champagne treatment."

. . . . .

Place the sugar cube in the bottom of a champagne flute. Douse with bitters, and lightly press until it crumbles. Top with sparkling wine or real French champagne.

{ Whiskey Bellini }

¾ ounce bourbon whiskey

¾ ounce Peach Purée
(Chapter 4)

3 ounces sparkling wine

¼ ounce peach brandy or
liqueur

The Bellini is a classic cocktail made from peach purée and sparkling wine. This recipe takes it one step further by adding a bit of bourbon to the mix (whiskey and peaches are amazing together). This feminine drink is fruity enough for a lady but strong enough for a woman!

• • • • •

Pour bourbon and Peach Purée into a cocktail shaker. Add ice, shake well, and strain into a champagne flute. Top with sparkling wine. Float (drizzle in) the peach brandy or liqueur, then serve.

{ Tipple Thyme }

1½ ounces blood orange juice

½ ounce fresh lemon juice

¾ ounce Thyme Syrup (Chapter 4)

3 ounces sparkling wine

GARNISH: lemon twist or sprig of thyme

As a thoughtful entertainer, it's important to consider nonalcoholic options for guests who don't drink liquor. This bubbly libation can be made with regular sparkling wine or you can substitute Fre Alcohol Removed Brut for a booze-free grape-based alternative. Whether making drinks with or without alcohol, always use fresh juices and the best quality ingredients possible!

• • • • •

Pour juices and syrup into a champagne flute. Top with sparkling wine. Garnish with lemon twist or thyme sprig.

{ Italian 75 }

1 ounce gin

½ ounce lemon juice

½ ounce Lavender-
Rosemary Syrup
(Chapter 4)

3 ounces sparkling
Lambrusco frizzante

GARNISH: Candied Lemon
(Chapter 6)

The original classic French 75 is made with gin, fresh lemon juice, simple syrup, and sparkling wine. A twist on that formula, this Italian-inspired version switches out simple syrup for a homemade herbal one and tops the drink with sparkling lambrusco instead of plain sparkling wine. Get creative and try your own!

· · · · ·

Pour gin, lemon juice, and rosemary syrup into a cocktail shaker. Add ice, shake well, and strain into a champagne coupe (or small wine glass). Top with sparkling red Italian Lambrusco. Garnish with a Candied Lemon.

{ Cherry Kiss }

2 teaspoons white
granulated sugar for rim

1 ounce brandy

1 ounce ruby port

¾ ounce Cherry Heering
liqueur

¼ ounce nutty liqueur
(Frangelico or Trader Vic's
Macadamia Nut Liqueur)

GARNISH: 1 "drunken" black
cherry (soaked in brandy for
at least 4 hours) for garnish

The richness of brandy and port complement each other beautifully in this cocktail. All you have to do to take this recipe over the top is to add a bit of cherry liqueur. This drink has a very classic feel and is ideal when served as an after-dinner treat.

· · · · ·

Rim a glass with white granulated sugar, set aside. Stir all liquid ingredients, with ice. Gently strain into glass. Drop drunken cherry into the bottom of drink, allowing it to sink to the bottom.

{ Garden Bloom }

1 strawberry

½ ounce fresh lemon juice

¾ ounce Lavender-
Rosemary Syrup
(Chapter 4)

2 ounce Sauvignon Blanc

¾ ounce Grey Goose La Poire
(pear-flavored vodka)

1 edible flower (for garnish)

A drink that delivers as much aroma as taste is a home run. This wine-based cocktail starts with Sauvignon Blanc, which is floral, and employs other beautiful garden-fresh ingredients that add their scent to the mix. This cocktail is virtually a bouquet in a glass.

・ ・ ・ ・ ・

Muddle strawberry with lemon juice. Add Lavender-Rosemary Syrup, Sauvignon Blanc, and vodka. Shake with ice. Double strain into an ice-filled white wine glass. Float edible flower on the surface of the drink.

Specialty Sangrias

If you've tried a wine-based cocktail, you've likely tried the Spanish wine punch called sangria. The best thing about this festive fiesta concoction is that there is really no wrong way to make it. Traditionally, it comprises chopped fruit, brandy, a bit of sugar, and inexpensive red wine. However, once you start feeling creative, the possibilities are endless! Here are some recipes to use as guidelines for your festivities, but feel free to break out some of your own twists.

{ Warm Winter Sangria }

2 oranges, sliced into rings

1 lemon, sliced into rings

¼ cup Honey Syrup (Chapter 4)

1 cup brandy

3 whole cloves

½ cup almond slivers

2 bottles Sutter Home Sweet Red

The smell of nuts, cloves, oranges, brandy, and red wine fills a home with the feeling of the holidays any time of year. This sangria-style wine punch can be served warm or cold, so although it's technically a "winter" sangria, it can be a great alternative in any season. This recipe serves twenty-four, just in case you have a full house for the holidays.

· · · · ·

1. Place sliced oranges and lemons into a large saucepan, reserving some for garnish. Drizzle with honey syrup, and add brandy, cloves, and almond slivers. Heat on low, and let simmer about 10 minutes.

2. Reduce heat and add one bottle of red wine. Let simmer about 5 minutes. Remove from heat; add second bottle of wine.

3. If serving warm, serve immediately in heat-resistant punch cups or wine glasses. If serving cold, refrigerate until cool, and serve over ice in wine glasses. Garnish with additional sliced lemons or oranges, if desired.

{ Sustainable Summer Sangria }

1½ cups diced organic
fruit, such as a mix of
strawberries, peaches,
plums

¼ cup Honey Syrup
(Chapter 4)

½ cup certified organic
vodka

½ cup peach juice (or nectar)

2 bottles organic white wine
(Sauvignon Blanc or pinot
grigio are particularly good
for this)

Sangria is the ultimate summer punch! And with warm weather entertaining, comes a bevy of backyard get-togethers, cookouts, and picnics. This organic cocktail serves twenty-four—because you never know how many people are going to show up on a hot summer's evening.

• • • • •

1. Place diced fruit into a glass bowl or plastic food storage container. Drizzle with honey syrup, vodka, and half the peach juice. Let marinate several hours. Refrigerate overnight for maximum flavor infusion.

2. When ready to serve, strain the juice from the fruit into a large pitcher. Save the fruit. Add remaining peach juice and all the wine to the juice in the large pitcher.

3. Spoon one bar spoon of marinated fruit mixture into each glass, fill with ice, and top with wine mixture.

{ Tropical Sangria }

1½ cups diced mix of pineapple and mango

¼ cup Pineapple Syrup (Chapter 4)

¼ cup fresh lime juice

½ cup cachaça (Brazilian sugar cane rum)

2 bottles Sauvignon Blanc

¼ cup Homemade Grenadine (Chapter 4)

Shredded coconut

Sangria can be made with any seasonal fruits, including tropical ones. In this recipe, mangoes, pineapple, rum, and a coconut garnish are incorporated into a white wine–based punch to please your guests at a pool party, backyard luau, or other summer celebration. This recipe serves twenty-four so you're sure to have enough.

· · · · ·

1. **TO MAKE THE SANGRIA:** Marinate chopped fruit in pineapple syrup, lime juice, and cachaça for a few hours in the refrigerator. When ready to serve, strain the liquid into a punch bowl or pitcher, and add the wine. Spoon a little marinated fruit into each coconut-rimmed glass. Fill with ice, then wine mixture.

2. **TO RIM GLASSES:** Pour some grenadine onto a plate and dip the rims of the wine glasses into the sticky liquid, then onto a plate of shredded coconut so that the coconut can stick to the glass rim. Set aside.

Seasonal Sparkling Sangria

1½ cups diced seasonal fruits: If summer, go for peaches, berries, cherries, kiwis. If winter, try pomegranate, kumquats, and other citrus fruits.

½ cup orange liqueur

½ cup Limoncello Della Casa (Chapter 5)

2 bottles sparkling wine

Festive drinks punctuate any celebration—and nothing says "congratulations" like a bit of bubbly. This sparkling sangria (which serves twenty-four guests) is a great way to toast the "bubbly bride" at a bridal shower, or to raise your glass at any other festive event that calls for some extra sparkle.

. . . . .

1. Marinate chopped fruit in orange liqueur and Limoncello Della Casa for several hours in the refrigerator.

2. When ready to serve, strain liquid (save fruit) into a punch bowl or pitcher, and top with sparkling wine. Place a bar spoon of fruit mixture into each glass. Add ice, and fill with sparkling wine mixture.

Allegria Sangria

2 apples, diced, skins on

2 Bosc pears, diced, skins on

1 cup red grapes, halved, skins on

½ cup homemade falernum syrup (found in specialty stores or online)

1 cup port

½ cup rye whiskey

½ cup spiced apple cider

2 bottles bold, red wine (California Zinfandel works well)

This sangria features autumn fruits, port, and a robust, spicy, Zinfandel red wine. Because of its bolder qualities, it can be equally appropriate at various kinds of parties. It's fun to serve with full-flavored foods at a backyard barbecue or a wintertime holiday celebration—and this sangria serves between twenty-four to thirty people so you won't run out!

. . . . .

Marinate the diced fruit in falernum syrup, port, and whiskey for a few hours in the refrigerator. When ready to serve, strain the liquid into a punchbowl or pitcher and reserve the fruit. Add cider and wine to the strained liquid. Spoon about a bar spoon of fruit mixture into each glass. Add ice, then fill with the spirit-and-wine mixture.

PaRtY WItH PReseRVes:

syrups, jams, purées, and shrubs

NOW THAT YOU KNOW HOW TO GROW YOUR OWN COCKTAIL GARDEN AND HOW TO NAVIGATE YOUR LOCAL FARMERS' MARKET, IT'S TIME TO TAKE A LOOK AT

how you can preserve the fruits of your labor. Here you'll learn how to make your own syrups, jams, jellies, and purées that will keep you drinking those delectable homegrown jewels for the whole year. For example, peaches are not seasonal at Christmastime (at least not in the Northern Hemisphere), so freezing a peach purée or popping open a jar of peach jam allows you to enjoy a taste of summer in your cocktail glass, whether it's sunny or snowy outside.

What is particularly fun about this chapter is that the syrup, purée, and jam recipes featured here can be used for eating and drinking. And while the creative ways you spread, drizzle, shake, or stir these ingredients depends entirely on your own imagination, you'll also find recipes that use these preserves to get you thinking in the right direction. So, break out grandma's apron because making—and mixing!—your own preserves is easier than you may think!

Syrups

Syrup is one of the most commonly used and important ingredients when creating a balanced cocktail; you want the ingredients to complement each other, without any particular element overshadowing the others. Syrups are traditionally sweet, and as mentioned earlier in this book, a bit of sweetness is integral to a cocktail because it brings out the flavor of fruits and rounds out spicy chili or tart citrus. Syrups also mix easily into a cocktail (versus granulated sugar) because it is already in liquid form.

Simple syrup (made of equal parts sugar and water) is the type most often called for in cocktail recipes. However, as you will see in the following syrup and drink recipes detailed here, bartenders and mixologists are exploring infused syrups as a way to bring more flavor to a drink. For example, agave syrup (made of equal parts agave nectar and water) or honey syrup (made of equal parts honey and water) adds not only sweetness to a cocktail, but dimension as well. You'll note that the measurements for the following basic syrup recipes (and the specialty syrups later on in this chapter) are provided in "parts" rather than cups or ounces. This allows you to make large quantities if you're hosting a large get-together, or a smaller batch if you're just having a few people over for a cocktail party. The ratios will stay the same no matter how much you make.

Not Just for Cocktails

The syrup recipes here are easily used in your culinary adventures, too! Try drizzling them on pancakes, cheeses, and desserts as well as in your cocktails.

{ Basic Simple Syrup }

1 part white granulated sugar

1 part water

Many cocktail recipes call for simple syrup, which is very easy to make. It is an efficient way to sweeten a cocktail because it is already in liquid form, and therefore does not leave grainy particles of sugar in the drink.

. . . . .

Bring both ingredients to a boil in a small saucepan, stirring constantly. Reduce heat, let simmer for a few minutes. Cool and store in a sealable bottle.

{ Rich Syrup }

2 parts white granulated sugar

1 part water

This is a more viscous version of simple syrup. Using a rich syrup can add a more concentrated sweetness with a bit more viscosity and body to a cocktail.

. . . . .

Bring both ingredients to a boil in a small saucepan, stirring constantly. Reduce heat, let simmer for a few minutes. Cool and store in a sealable bottle.

{ Rose or Orange Flower Syrups }

1 part rose water or orange
flower water

1 part white granulated sugar

Rose water and orange flower water are used in cocktails on their own, but you can also use them to make flavorful floral syrups for use in your cocktails. These exotic waters are most often found at ethnic grocery stores, and sometimes at high-end grocery or liquor stores.

• • • • •

Bring ingredients to a boil in a small saucepan, stirring constantly. Reduce heat, let simmer for a few minutes. Cool and store.

{ Homemade Grenadine }

2 parts fresh pomegranate
juice

2 parts white granulated
sugar

¼ part pomegranate
molasses

⅛ part orange flower water
(optional if not available)

Grenadine is called for in both alcoholic and nonalcoholic cocktails as a sweetening, flavoring, and coloring agent. This easy syrup tastes so much better than the mass produced, store-bought kind, so once you make it you will never want to settle for less.

• • • • •

1. Slowly heat pomegranate juice in a saucepan to medium heat without bringing to boil.

2. Add sugar and stir until dissolved.

3. Add pomegranate molasses and orange blossom water.

4. Cool. Pour into a sealable bottle and store.

{ Honey Syrup }

1 part honey

1 part water

Using honey adds both thickness and flavor to a syrup or cocktail. Farmers' markets and even grocery stores carry everything from lavender honey to wild-flower honey and beyond, so experiment with different flavors in your homemade cocktails to find a flavor you love. Play around with light and dark honeys to experience a different depth of flavor, as well.

. . . . .

Slowly heat honey and water into a small saucepan, stirring often, until nearly boiling. Let cool, then store in a sealable bottle. Refrigerate.

{ Ginger Honey Syrup }

2 parts honey

1 parts water

2 tablespoons fresh ginger, chopped

This recipe brings the added spice of ginger to the sweetness of natural honey. Experiment with different kinds of honey to complement the other ingredients you put into the cocktail.

. . . . .

Heat honey and water in a saucepan until thoroughly mixed. Reduce heat to low and add ginger. Remove from heat and let sit for 2 hours. Strain ginger, then bottle and refrigerate.

BEYOND BASICS: SPECIALTY SYRUPS

Most liquids can be used to make delicious syrups and you can experiment to make your syrups even more impressive. Whether you choose tea, fruit juice, or even wine, all sorts of flavorful liquids mixed with a sweetening agent add aroma, sugar, and depth to a cocktail. The following recipes show you how to create delicious syrups to use in cooking and cocktails. Feel free to substitute your own favorite ripe fruits, fresh herbs, or exotic teas for those suggested below to come up with your own specialty syrups.

Fresh Herb Syrups

If you want your herbal syrups to be more pungent, put healthy amounts of plucked leaves into the saucepan with equal parts sugar and water. If you prefer a more subtle flavor, you can adjust the recipes by using a smaller quantity of herbs according to your taste. One rule of thumb to keep in mind when muddling herbs directly into cocktails or cooking them into syrups, is not to include the plant stem. It adds an unpleasant bitterness that can be avoided by using only the leaves and flowers of an edible plant.

{ Thyme Syrup }

1 cup sugar

1 cup water

25 leaves plucked off the stem of a thyme plant

Thyme has been used throughout history in everything from food to incense. Its hearty fragrance and flavor make it an intriguing addition to cocktails—particularly when it's paired with citrus fruits. With regard to spirits, it mixes especially well with gin.

· · · · ·

Bring the above to a boil in a saucepan, stirring occasionally. Reduce heat to low. Simmer on low for 10 minutes. Let cool. Double strain into a glass jar or bottle. Let cool. Refrigerate.

{ Mint Syrup }

1 cup water

1 cup white granulated sugar, or raw sugar

12–15 freshly plucked mint leaves

Not only useful as an extra flavor-booster in sweetening mojitos and mint juleps, mint syrup is wonderful when paired with nearly every kind of light or dark spirit. It is also astoundingly delicious when used with fresh-muddled fruits such as strawberries.

· · · · ·

Bring all the above to a boil in a saucepan, stirring occasionally. Reduce heat to low. Simmer on low for 10 minutes. Let cool. Double strain into a glass jar or bottle. Refrigerate.

{ Lavender-Rosemary Syrup }

1 cup brewed lavender tea
(found in specialty tea shops,
gourmet grocery stores,
or dry your own lavender
flowers)

1 cup white granulated sugar

Approximately 25 leaves
plucked from fresh rosemary
sprigs

Rosemary is one of the most fabulous herbs to use in both cooking and cocktails. Whether muddled in the bottom of a mixing glass, set on fire as a smoking garnish, or incorporated into a syrup, it adds an earthy layer of herbal flavoring which works particularly in gin, vodka, and tequila cocktails. In this recipe, lavender tea replaces plain water, which further enhances its flavor.

· · · · ·

Bring all of the above to a boil in a saucepan, stirring occasionally. Reduce heat to low. Simmer on low for 10 minutes. Let cool. Double strain into a glass jar or bottle. Refrigerate.

{ Smoked-Sage Syrup }

12 fresh sage leaves

1 cup water

¾ cup agave nectar
(found at gourmet grocers
and health food stores)

The smoke from sage is used to cleanse spirits in some Native American and New Age practices. In cocktails, smoked sage brings an ethereal-yet-earthy quality to the kinds of spirits used in cocktails! This syrup is fun to experiment with in both culinary and cocktail-ian endeavors.

· · · · ·

1. Hold the base of the sage leaves with a couple of fingers, and with the other hand, light their tips aflame using a lighter.

2. Allow the leaves to burn until the tips are charred, then drop them, along with the water and agave nectar, into a small saucepan. Bring to a boil, stirring occasionally.

3. Reduce heat to low. Simmer on low for 10 minutes. Let cool. Double strain into a glass jar or bottle. Refrigerate.

{ Lemon-Basil Syrup }

1¼ cups sugar

1 cup water

¼ cup fresh lemon juice

10 leaves plucked off
the stem of a basil plant
(a lemon basil plant
would be ideal)

Basil is a versatile staple when you're working with cocktails; it can be muddled in a cocktail shaker or cooked into a syrup. It works particularly well with lemon, so this syrup is an especially easy ingredient to use in vodka- and gin-based drinks.

. . . . .

Bring all the above to a boil, stirring occasionally. Reduce heat to low. Simmer on low for 10 minutes. Let cool for about 30 minutes to infuse the flavors. Double strain into a glass jar or bottle. Let cool. Refrigerate.

{ Hibiscus Syrup }

1 cup water

¼ cup dried hibiscus flowers

1 tablespoon grated fresh
ginger

1 cup sugar

3 drops vanilla extract

This floral syrup appears in the Flor de Jamaica cocktail in Chapter 7. It is wonderful not only with tequila but also vodka, gin, and whiskey—and when drizzled into a sparkling cocktail.

. . . . .

1. Bring water to a boil in a saucepan; add flowers and ginger, and reduce heat. Simmer for 10 minutes. Let stand for 2 hours to infuse.

2. Strain the flowers and ginger, and pour infused water back in a saucepan and add sugar. Stir over low heat until all sugar is dissolved, then add vanilla. Let cool.

3. Pour into a sealable bottle. Refrigerate.

WINE SYRUPS

As explored in the "Grape to Glass" chapter of this book, wine is a wonderful base in sangrias and other kinds of punches, as well as poured as a straight ingredient in various cocktails. However, when you use wine as a base for syrups, it opens up a whole new way of thinking about it for use in mixed drinks. The flavors and aromas in wine translate beautifully into syrups because they bring a unique depth of flavor and fruitiness without adding as much sugar as juices do. These syrups work wonderfully in both wine-based and spirit-based cocktails.

{ Red Wine Syrup }

1 part wine (use big, flavorful reds such as Cabernet, Zinfandel, Shiraz, or Malbec)

1 part granulated white sugar

Red wine brings dimension to a drink both when used directly in a cocktail or in syrups. Experiment with raw sugar as well as white granulated in the recipe below to explore varying flavor options.

· · · · ·

Bring wine and sugar to a boil in a saucepan, stirring constantly. Remove from heat immediately. Cool, stirring occasionally. Store in an airtight glass bottle. Refrigerate.

{ Hibiscus Cabernet Syrup }

1 cup brewed hibiscus tea
(found in many grocery
stores and tea houses)

1½ cups Cabernet Sauvignon
wine

2 cups white granulated
sugar

*This syrup uses both tea and wine, the combination of which will create a rich
and layered flavor profile in your cocktail. It also works well with tequila as seen
in the Flaming Angelico cocktail found in Chapter 3.*

. . . . .

Pour all ingredients into a medium-sized saucepan. Slowly bring to a boil,
stirring almost constantly. Immediately remove from heat, let cool. Store in
an airtight glass bottle. Refrigerate.

{ Lemongrass-Sauvignon Blanc Syrup }

1 whole stem lemongrass,
cut into ½ inch long pieces
(found at gourmet groceries
and Asian markets)

1 cup white granulated sugar

1½ cups Sauvignon Blanc
wine

*Sauvignon Blanc is a crisp, fresh, light wine. When infused with lemongrass in this
syrup, it becomes a superb ingredient for vodka-, gin-, and sake-based cocktails.*

. . . . .

Place all ingredients in a medium-sized saucepan. Slowly bring to a boil,
stirring almost constantly. Reduce heat, let sit for 10 minutes while cooling.
Strain and store in a sealable bottle for up to 2 weeks if refrigerated.

JUICE-BASED SYRUPS

The natural sweetness of fruit juices makes them idea for syrup bases. As you're cooking, keep in mind that the amount of sugar used to create these syrups can also be reduced slightly if you're using very sweet or very ripe, freshly juiced fruits. Tart fruit juices could require a bit more sugar. Adjusting these syrup recipes to your own taste buds is entirely acceptable when it comes to experimenting with flavor and balance.

{ Cherry-Cinnamon Syrup }

2 cups cherry juice

2 cups white granulated sugar

1 whole cinnamon stick

This fruit and spice combination is great all year, but it's particularly enticing around the holidays. (Add a couple of whole cloves to the pot and the mix is Christmas in a cocktail syrup.) In addition to using this syrup in drinks, consider drizzling it over yellow cake, or mixing it into a vanilla milkshake for a decadent treat.

· · · · ·

Bring all ingredients to a boil in a saucepan, stirring often. Lower heat and simmer 3–5 minutes. Let cool. Store in refrigerator for up to 2 weeks.

{ Hot Passion Fruit Syrup }

1 cup sugar

1 cup water

½ cup passion fruit pulp and juice (or passion fruit purée)

1 jalapeño, chopped—take the tops and bottoms off, but don't remove the seeds

Vodka or cachaça (optional)

The pulp and juice of the passion fruit used to create this delicious syrup come from scooping out the inside of the fruit. This syrup is a great way to capture the unique tart-sweet flavor of the passion fruit year-round, if you can get hold of some when they are in season to make this syrup. If not, look for passion fruit purée, which is available online and in gourmet stores.

. . . . .

Pour all ingredients into a medium-sized saucepan, and stir over low heat, until all the sugar is dissolved (about 10 minutes). Let stand for 30 minutes to cool, and then strain to remove the passion fruit seeds and jalapeño. Pour into a sterilized, sealable glass bottle. The syrup will keep for about a month if refrigerated. Add a splash of vodka or cachaça if you want the alcohol to help preserve it even longer.

{ Jalapeño Syrup }

1 cup sugar

1 cup water

2 jalapeños, roughly chopped—take the tops and bottoms off, but don't remove the seeds

The kick of different kinds of chilies enhances both cocktails and cooking because the jalapeño has not only spice but a fresh herbal flavor that lends itself to food and drink The chili makes this syrup a natural with Mexican tequila (particularly silver or unaged tequila) but think about it for other white, spirit-based cocktails. If you want to try this syrup in your cooking, try it drizzled on brownies and vanilla ice cream. It's curiously delicious there, too!

. . . . .

Combine all in a medium-sized saucepan. Slowly bring to a boil, stirring constantly until all the sugar is dissolved. Remove from heat, and let stand for about 30 minutes while cooling. Double strain into a sealable bottle. Refrigerate.

{ Ginger-Lemon Syrup }

5–7 slices of peeled fresh
ginger cut about ¼ inch thick

Zest of three lemons

1 cup water

1 cup sugar

Ginger is a fantastic ingredient in cocktails and desserts—whether it's candied, muddled fresh, or cooked into a syrup. It has some natural sweetness as well as lots of spicy zing. This syrup is great with gin, vodka, rum, and whiskey.

· · · · ·

Place all ingredients into a medium-sized saucepan. Bring to a slow boil, stirring often. Remove from heat. Let sit about 30 minutes while cooling. Double strain and store in a sealable bottle. Refrigerate.

{ Rhubarb and Fennel Syrup }

1 cup chopped fresh, red
rhubarb

½ cup chopped fresh organic
fennel bulbs

1 cup water

1 cup white, granulated
sugar

1 pinch of kosher salt

This syrup brings the vegetables from the kitchen into the bar and is used in the Sotto Voce in Chapter 7. Once you're done mixing up that cocktail, try this ingredient in a fresh rhubarb pie!

· · · · ·

Combine ingredients in a heavy bottomed pot. Simmer over low heat until all color and flavor is extracted from the rhubarb and the fennel. Strain the syrup through cheesecloth. Store in an airtight bottle. Refrigerate.

{ Bangkok Lemongrass-Agave Syrup }

1 cup agave nectar

¼ cup fresh lemongrass

2 vanilla bean pods

¼ cup Candied Lime
(Chapter 6)

⅛ cup citrus flowers
(optional ingredient, if
available. These can be
found at a farmers' market or
backyard tree, depending on
where you live.)

The fresh, citrusy aroma and taste of this syrup is so versatile that it works well with most spirits. Using agave nectar as a base is not only a healthful alternative to white sugar but also brings more flavor to the forefront of the cocktail.

· · · · ·

Bring all ingredients to a simmer in a saucepan. Remove from heat and immediately seal in an airtight jar or bottle. Freeze mixture for a week. After that time, add ½ cup water, stir, and filter or strain until no residue is left. Store in the refrigerator up to 2 weeks.

{ Lemon-Lime Syrup }

½ cup fresh lime or
lemon juice
(you can also combine
both lemon and lime)

½ cup lime or water
(left over from blanching
lemon and lime wheels for
garnishes)

1 cup granulated white sugar

This very versatile syrup is the by-product of the Candied Limes described in Chapter 6. After blanching the citrus wheels and removing them to dry, save the water that they were cooked in to make this delicious syrup.

· · · · ·

Place all ingredients into a medium-sized saucepan. Bring to a boil, stirring constantly. Reduce heat and let simmer for 10 minutes. Cool; pour into sealable bottles and store for up to 2 weeks in the refrigerator.

{ Pineapple Syrup }

1 cup fresh pineapple juice
(canned will do if fresh
pineapples are not available)

1 cup white granulated sugar

This tropical juice syrup is fantastic when mixed into "tiki" rum-based drinks, as well as other creative twists on modern and classic cocktails. Pineapples grow on islands and in exotic locales, the same sorts of places from which rum hails, so the pairing of sweet, pungent, flavorful pineapple is perfect with rum. However, don't be afraid to try it elsewhere—it is tasty in just about any kind of cocktail.

. . . . .

Skin and juice pineapple. Strain out fibrous bits of fruit through a fine sieve or cheesecloth. Pour juice and sugar into a saucepan and bring to a boil, stirring often. Reduce heat and let simmer for 10–15 minutes. Cool; pour into a sealable bottle and store for up to 2 weeks in the refrigerator.

Jams, Jellies, and More!

Not only are jams and marmalades great ways to preserve seasonal fruit for use throughout the year but they bring a certain rich body to the cocktail. They are also bursting with flavor and freshness that complement the citrus, molasses, herbal, or spicy notes of various spirits. There are a variety of ways that you can make sure your fruits and veggies are preserved:

○ **PRESERVES:** In this process fruit is cooked with sugar to the point where large chunks of fruit or whole fruit, such as berries, are suspended in a syrup base. The texture of preserves is not smooth like jelly or jam.

○ **JAM:** Jam is made from crushed or chopped fruit cooked with sugar, and sometimes pectin (see recipe below) and citrus juice. Jam often has fruit pulp in it but not usually large chunks of fruit. If it is made from more than one fruit, or includes nuts or raisins, it is considered a conserve.

○ **JELLY:** Jelly is clearer, brighter, and firmer than jam. It typically consists of fruit juice, sugar, pectin, and some form of citrus (usually lemon) juice.

○ **MARMALADE:** Marmalade is a soft jelly, usually citrus based (lemon, lime, bitter orange, grapefruit), and includes the flesh and peel of the fruit. The peel gives it a little bitterness, which makes it interesting in cocktails, too.

○ **CONSERVE:** Conserve can be a mixture of more than one fruit in a jam. It can also be whole small fruits preserved in a syrup or jelly.

○ **FRUIT CURD:** Fruit curd is a creamier fruit spread combining sugar, eggs, and butter.

Now that you know what you'll be making, what do you need to know to actually cook up a batch of jam, jelly, or other preserve? Read on . . .

PECTIN

Pectin thickens the fruit mixtures for jams and jellies, and helps them to jell, so it is often required when making fruit preserves. Some fruits, apples, plums, and grapes for example, contain enough naturally occurring pectin that they don't need more added. However, other fruits, including most berries, need either to be mixed with fruits containing high amounts of natural pectin, or have supplemental pectin added to the recipe.

{ Pectin }

2 pounds of apple cores and skin peelings, from roughly 4 pounds of apples

Water (enough to cover cores and skins), roughly 4 cups

Fortunately, it is not difficult to make your own pectin from scratch, but if making your own doesn't tickle your fancy, you can purchase pectin in powdered or liquid form at the store.

· · · · · ·

1. Place about 2 pounds of apple cores and skin peelings into a pot. (Save the rest of the apple "meat" to make apple sauce or a pie, or infuse into a spirit such as whiskey by placing apple slices into a large glass jar, filling it with whiskey and letting it sit for a week, then straining through cheesecloth.)

2. Cover the apple cores and skins with water and slowly simmer them for 30 minutes.

3. Strain through cheesecloth and set aside the liquid.

4. Place the pulpy matter back into the pot, cover it with water, and slowly simmer on low heat for another 30 minutes.

5. Strain as described above.

6. Mix equal parts of both batches of liquid, mix them together in a saucepan, and bring them back to a simmer on low heat until about ¼ of it evaporates.

7. Remove from the heat and allow to cool. Refrigerate and use for up to 1 week, or store in a sterilized, airtight container for up to a year.

STORE YOUR PRESERVES

Rule number one when preparing to start the jamming process is to have plenty of sterile jars; if they are not properly cleaned and sterilized, the contents will quickly spoil from lingering bacteria and contaminants. Unless you are making large quantities of jams, jellies, etc., buy small jars so that you can open them as needed, and keep unused portions in the fridge for a few days without having a whole pot of jam spoil if not consumed right away. To sterilize your jars in your kitchen, try one of the following methods:

○ **BOILING:** If you have a stovetop, place your jars in a large pot and cover them with luke-warm water. Then slowly bring the water to a boil. It's best to bring the jars to a boil this way, rather than drop them into boiling water as the sudden temperature change could break the glass. Boil the jars for about 10 minutes, making sure to turn them if any part is exposed. When done, turn off the heat and immediately remove the steaming jars with kitchen tongs. Place them on a cooling rack, open side up, and then fill them with the warm fruit mixture. Seal them closed, cool completely, and then store.

○ **BAKING:** Line a baking pan with cooking parchment paper (or newspaper) and place the jars, open side up, upon them. Preheat the oven to about 350°F or 180°C, and bake the jars for about 25 minutes. Remove one jar at a time, filling it with warm fruit mixture. Seal, close, and store.

○ **MICROWAVE:** It is also possible to sterilize clean, wet jars in the microwave for 1 minute on a high setting. Remove hot jars with an oven mitt, and immediately fill with warm fruit mixture. Seal, close, and store.

Now that you know what you need, it's time to start preserving your fruits!

PARTY WITH PRESERVES

Here are some jam, curd, and marmalade recipes that are delicious on their own and are also intriguing to shake into cocktails. Use these preserves to bring a unique element of sweetness and viscosity to your drinks. And once you get the hang of the process, experiment with your own ingredients and combinations. There's nothing better than getting creative in the kitchen with your home garden or farmers' market finds and then bringing that tasty joy to your cocktail shaker!

{ Spiced-Wine Jelly }

1 bottle red wine

1 cinnamon stick

3 whole cloves

6 peppercorns

½ teaspoon nutmeg

½ teaspoon powdered ginger
(or three ½-inch slices fresh,
unpeeled ginger)

1¾ cups raw sugar

Zest of 1 lemon

Zest of ½ medium-sized
orange (blood orange is
preferable)

1 ounce homemade Pectin
(see recipe in this chapter)

This wine-based jelly is amazing when shaken into a cocktail; try it with mezcal (a smoky agave spirit in the tequila family) or an herbaceous gin—it's sublime. It's also delicious when served as a condiment on a gourmet cheese plate

· · · · ·

Place the wine, spices, ginger, zests, and sugar into a medium-sized saucepan and bring to a boil, stirring often. Reduce heat and let mixture simmer on low until it becomes syrupy in texture, stirring often. Add the pectin, stir, let simmer a few minutes. Cool, pour into sterilized jam jars, and store.

{ Lime Marmalade }

2½ pounds limes

1 medium-sized orange

1 medium-sized lemon

8½ cups water

5 pounds white sugar

The seeds of two vanilla pods
(Heilala from Tonga is the
most fragrant vanilla on
earth)

Making marmalade is a lot easier than it seems. This marmalade is perfect to spread on pound cake or fluffy toast and it's an integral ingredient in the Brazilian Breakfast recipe in Chapter 7.

. . . . .

1. Peel the zest of the limes, lemon, and orange, then slice thinly and place the peels in a large saucepan with the water to soften them.

2. Juice all the citrus, and strain the juice through a strainer to remove all the seeds and any pith, and add to the pan.

3. Chop half the juiced fruit, and tie into a cheesecloth bag, and put in the pan with the zests and juice, over a low heat, until all the zests are very soft.

4. Preheat the oven to 350°F.

5. Strain all the liquid from the cheesecloth bag into the pan, and discard bag.

6. Bring the fruit/juice to a boil, turn down to a simmer, and add the sugar and vanilla seeds, stirring well to dissolve the sugar.

7. Bring to the boil again, and cook for 10–15 minutes until the mixture reaches setting point. The best way to test is to put a little on a chilled saucer or spoon, and run your finger through. If it leaves a trail, it's set.

8. Let stand until thickened. Remove the vanilla beans, and stir the mixture well. Ladle it into sterilized jars, and seal until ready to use.

{ Fig and Whiskey Preserve }

2 pounds of figs

2 cups of sugar

1 cup water

1 cup whiskey

Juice of 1 lemon

This jam is not only sublime for cocktails, such as The Whiskied Fig cocktail in Chapter 7, but it's also gorgeous when served as an accompaniment to artisanal cheeses and fresh bread. Your guests will be surprised to taste your homemade jam both as an appetizer and in your hand-crafted cocktails . . . and it's a great conversation starter for a party!

• • • • •

1. Wash the figs well, then cut them into quarters.

2. Slowly heat the sugar and water in a small saucepan until the sugar is dissolved.

3. Add the figs and bring to a boil for about 5 minutes, stirring constantly.

4. Add the lemon and whiskey, cover, and simmer on low for about 30 minutes.

5. Cool, pour into jars, seal, and store.

{ Lemon and Mandarin Curd }

1 cup white, granulated sugar

3 eggs

Finely grated rind and juice of 1½ lemons

Finely grated rind and juice of 1½ mandarins

2 sticks unsalted butter, melted

The addition of sugar, eggs, and butter turn a fruit preserve into a curd. This recipe brings silky texture and bright flavor to any cocktail you use it in, such as the Temptation Gage recipe found in Chapter 7.

· · · · ·

1. In a bowl, whisk together the sugar and eggs until smooth. Stir in strained juice, rind, and butter.

2. Cook in the microwave for 1-minute intervals, stirring after each minute until the mixture is thick enough to coat the back of a metal spoon, about 10 minutes.

3. Remove from the microwave, and pour into small sterile jars. Store for up to 3 weeks in the refrigerator.

{ Strawberry-Rhubarb Jelly }

¾ cup chopped rhubarb

1½ cups ripe strawberries, tops removed

½ teaspoon balsamic vinegar

1½ cups sugar

2 ounces homemade Pectin (recipe in this chapter)

Strawberries and rhubarb are a natural combination because the sweetness from the ripe berries offsets the tartness of the rhubarb. A drizzle of balsamic vinegar gives this combination an extra kick of flavor. This jelly mixes well with tequila, gin, and vodka when shaken into cocktails. Also try muddling a bit of fresh mint into the cocktail shaker with this combo and you'll be over the moon!

· · · · ·

1. Wash and cut rhubarb into 1-inch pieces and chop in a food processor or blender. Add strawberries; blend together. Strain mixture through a cheesecloth and collect juice. (This should yield about 1½ cups.)

2. Pour juice into a medium-sized saucepan. Add balsamic vinegar and sugar and mix well. Bring to a boil, stirring constantly. Add pectin. Bring to a full, rolling boil for 1 minute, stirring constantly.

3. Remove from heat, skim off any foam, and pour into sterilized, half-pint jars. (Leave ¼-inch space at the top of the jars.)

Purées

As with fruit preserves, purées—smooth mixtures of fruits or vegetables which have been finely mashed or blended into a velvety paste—are used for both cooking and cocktails. Purées are thicker than jams and jellies but can be preserved in jam jars in the same way to prolong the use of the farm-fresh, seasonal fruits. Here are a few simple examples to get you started.

{ Peach Purée }

4–5 ripe peaches

1 tablespoon lemon juice

¼ cup raw sugar

Pinch cinnamon

½ cup water

Peach Purée is an integral ingredient in a classic Bellini cocktail (made up of peach purée and champagne). However, peaches also play nicely with bourbon, tequila, brandy, and gin. Although you can keep a container of fresh peach purée in a sealed container in the refrigerator, also consider filling an ice cube tray and freezing little cubes of purée, so that it is always on hand for great cocktails any time!

· · · · ·

1. Skin and remove the pits from the peaches. Cut them into chunks, and place them, along with the other ingredients, in a medium-sized saucepan. Bring to a low simmer for about 10 minutes. Let cool, then purée in a blender.

2. Store in a jar or plastic container for a few days in the refrigerator. (You can also dollop spoonfuls of peach purée into ice cube trays or place ½-cup quantities into freezer bags to store frozen, small-quantity servings.)

{ Persimmon Purée }

¾ cup sugar

3 cups water

4 Fuyu persimmons, chopped
(do not substitute other
persimmon types)

1 fresh vanilla bean, split
down the middle to open

2 tablespoons crystallized
ginger, cut into small cubes

1 pinch nutmeg

Juice of 1 lemon

This purée is absolutely delicious on its own, whether spread on bread, or shaken into the Golden Gate cocktail (Chapter 7). Persimmons, like most fruits, are seasonal. Therefore, it is highly recommended to make persimmon purée when the fruits are available so you can enjoy their flavor in cooking and cocktails, year round.

· · · · ·

1. In a medium-sized saucepan, melt sugar over medium to medium-high heat until amber or golden brown, stirring occasionally to avoid burning. Once color is achieved, remove from heat and pour water slowly down the sides of the pot. Water will bubble, steam, and sputter and sugar will immediately harden.

2. Return to medium-high heat and cook until sugar is melted again, stirring occasionally. Once completely melted, add chopped persimmons, vanilla bean, and crystallized ginger. Cook on medium-low heat (strong simmer) for about 2 hours, or until persimmons are completely soft and liquid is reduced by about half. Stir in a pinch of nutmeg. Remove from heat and cool.

3. Once cooled, remove vanilla bean, then scrape any remaining pulp from inside the bean and put into mixture. Discard vanilla bean pod.

4. Pour lemon juice into the mixture then pour purée into a sieve strainer. Hold strainer over a large bowl and use the back of a large spoon to press and stir the purée solids against the sieve, extracting a finer liquid and leaving thicker solids in the strainer. Use the fine liquid purée to make the cocktail. The remaining thick purée in the strainer can be jarred for a few days and used as a delicious jam on toast or muffins.

{ Pumpkin Purée }

1 smallish pumpkin

This delicious purée is wonderful on its own as a side dish, baked into a pie, whipped into pumpkin butter, or shaken (with rum or whiskey) into a cocktail. Obviously, in the United States, pumpkin is a staple when thinking about wintertime (Thanksgiving and Christmas) entertaining, so keep this ingredient in mind around that time of year.

· · · · ·

1. Slice off the top of the pumpkin (the part with the stalk). Cut the pumpkin in half and remove the seeds.

2. Preheat oven to 350°F. Place the pieces on a baking sheet and bake until light golden brown and soft (about 30–40 minutes). The skin will be crinkly and peel off easily.

3. Scoop the cooled pumpkin meat into a food processor (or blender). If the mixture is dry, add a little water. When blended into a creamy consistency, spoon into jam jars and seal. (You can also freeze small servings in freezer bags as an alternative method of storage.)

{ Carrot- and Beet-Gingered Purée }

2½ cups peeled, chopped carrots

½ cup peeled, chopped beets

¼ cup peeled, chopped fresh ginger

1 cup sugar

¾ cup water

Zest of 1 lemon (save the juice)

1 tablespoon honey

This mixture is not only healthy and tasty as a side dish in a meal but also as a unique ingredient mixed into a citrusy gin-based cocktail. The accessibility of the ingredients also makes it an easy one to add to your kitchen and cocktail repertoire.

· · · · ·

1. Place carrots, beets, ginger, lemon zest, and sugar into a medium sized saucepan with water. Cover and bring to a boil, stirring occasionally. Remove from heat.

2. Let cool and remove the lemon zest. Blend the carrots, beets, and ginger in a food processor or blender.

3. Return to saucepan and cook on low for about 30 minutes, stirring often. Add the honey and lemon juice. Cook for an additional 5 minutes. Let cool, store in jam jars.

{ Prickly Pear Purée }

1 cup peeled, chopped
prickly pear chunks
(about 4 prickly pears)

2 tablespoons white,
granulated sugar

¼ cup water

In the Southwestern United States, yummy things like cactus candy and prickly pear margaritas (both of which employ prickly pear purée) are relatively common. However, prickly pears also grow in other parts of the world. While some people may not be well acquainted with the Nopales cacti and their red "prickly pear" fruits in other parts of the world, they are sometimes available in Mexican or gourmet grocers—and are well worth preparing and storing if you come across some.

. . . . .

1. Remove any remaining thorns from the whole prickly pear fruit, wash well, remove skins, and cut into quarters. (How to peel the prickly pear: Cut off the ends of the fruit. Slice it vertically and peel off its skin.)

2. Simmer the prickly pears in water and sugar for 10–15 minutes in a medium-sized saucepan, allowing some of the water to slowly evaporate. Stir almost constantly. Remove from heat.

3. When cool, place all contents of the pan into a food processor or blender and blend until smooth. Strain through a sieve. Pour into a jam jar and store. (You can also freeze small servings in freezer bags as an alternative method of storage.)

Shrubs

We are not talking about bushes from the "Garden to Glass" chapter here. A shrub is another old-time way to preserve fruits and vegetables. Shrubs essentially consist of fruit, vinegar, and sugar, and when applied to mixology, shrubs bring a bit of acidic kick to a cocktail. Different kinds of vinegar bring different elements to the shrub. Some are made with red wine vinegar, cider vinegar, balsamic vinegar . . . the possibilities are only as limited as your imagination. Shrubs are still not common in mainstream mixology—yet!—but below are a few recipes to help you get thinking about these unique ingredients.

{ Berry Shrub }

1 cup blackberries

1 cup raspberries

1 cup sugar

¾ cup red wine vinegar

This shrub utilizes fresh berries, which are best when gathered in season. If you have an absolute hankering to make this recipe when they are not available, try frozen berries as an alternative. This shrub appears in the Damian's Diapason cocktail in Chapter 7.

• • • • •

1. Combine everything but vinegar in a saucepan and place over medium heat stirring frequently until sugar melts and berries break down. Reduce heat to low and add vinegar; then simmer for 2 minutes.

2. Remove from heat and let stand covered at room temp for 6 hours or overnight. Strain through cheesecloth or a fine mesh strainer and then bottle.

{ Blueberry and Black Cherry-Balsamic Shrub }

1 cup blueberries

1 cup pitted black cherries

1 cup raw sugar

¼ cup dark rum
(Gosling's is preferable)

1 cup balsamic vinegar

The pungent earthiness of balsamic vinegar calls for bold fruits such as black cherries and blueberries. Adding a little dark rum intensifies the flavors even further. This shrub is strong and delicious when used sparingly to punch up a hearty cocktail.

. . . . .

1. Mix the blueberries, cherries, and sugar into a large glass jar. Muddle them slightly to mix flavors and release juices. Add the vinegar and rum, and let sit overnight.

2. Pour all contents of the jar into a medium-sized saucepan and heat, stirring constantly until nearly boiling. Reduce heat, let cool, and double strain (or strain through cheesecloth) to remove all fruit pulp. Store in a sealable bottle.

{ Carambola (Star Fruit) Shrub }

1 cup chopped carambola
(seasonally found in ethnic
and gourmet grocers)

1 cup granulated white sugar

¼ cup dry sake

1 cup rice wine vinegar

This is a fun shrub to use in Asian-inspired cocktails, because the starfruit comes from that part of the world and their sweet-yet-tart juiciness makes them ideal for shrubs. Try this ingredient in a sake-based cocktail or perhaps with cachaça, a Brazilian sugarcane rum.

. . . . .

1. Mix fruit and sugar into a large glass jar. Muddle slightly, then add the vinegar and sake, and let sit overnight.

2. Pour all contents of the jar into a medium-sized saucepan and heat, stirring constantly until nearly boiling. Reduce heat, let cool, and double strain (or strain through cheesecloth) to remove all fruit pulp. Store in a sealable bottle.

CHAPTER 5

MIXING It UP:
Infusions, Meat, Dairy, Eggs, Liqueurs, and Bitters

IN ADDITION TO FALLING BACK ON THE
EARTH'S BOUNTY OF FRUITS, VEGETABLES, AND
HERBS AND YOUR OWN NEWFOUND CULINARY GENIUS WITH
jams and jellies, make your edible cocktails something to talk about by
including unexpected ingredients like meats, dairy, eggs, bitters, and more!
This is where the alchemy of cocktails comes into play, where being a bartender, gourmet chef, and mad scientist collide. In this chapter, you'll learn
how to infuse spirits with many things (including meat!) and make your own
liqueurs (sweet, viscous, fruity, nutty, or herbal alcoholic sippers that can be
enjoyed on their own or incorporated into cocktails). If it sounds daunting,
don't worry. Cocktails are fun—and you're going to love getting creative and
thinking out of the box.

Infusions

With a little bit of preparation, a few tools, and a few weeks to let the ingredients sit, you can bring the flavors of fresh herbs, flowers, roots, nuts, fruits, trees, and even meat into your edible cocktails. Sound bizarre? It is! And, that's why infusions are so much fun. You can take a bottle of booze you already like and give it a flavor boost by allowing an organic material (from the ground, a bush, or a tree) to sit in alcohol long enough to infuse its flavors into it. By infusing your own spirits, you're in control of how it tastes. You can give your booze a subtle hint of spice or a deep, aromatic enhancement. So, as you're creating the following infusions, keep in mind that the longer you let an infusion sit, the more intense its flavor will become. So, once you reach the desired result, remove whatever you are using to infuse the spirit, then bottle, and store your "edible" elixir.

{ Rosemary-Infused Reposado Tequila }

3 sprigs fresh, organic
rosemary

1 bottle reposado tequila
(750 ml)

This wonderful infusion of rosemary brings out some of the aromatic, herbal qualities in reposado (slightly aged) tequila. This infusion is not only fabulous for margaritas but also other tequila-based cocktails.

· · · · ·

Place rosemary in bottle and let sit for about 2 weeks. At that point, the rosemary can be removed. If you leave the sprigs in the tequila, it will continue to infuse and become more concentrated. Strain out any solids. Bottle and store.

{ Pine-Infused Gin }

1 4-inch cutting from a
pine tree

1 bottle gin (750 ml)

Bring the aromatic experience of a walk in the woods right into your cocktail glass by infusing pine needles into a bottle of gin. Be sure to wash the pine tree cutting well with water, and maybe even give it a wipe with an alcohol-soaked cloth to sanitize it before placing it into the bottle.

· · · · ·

Wash the pine cutting thoroughly; then place it into the bottle of gin. Let it sit for about 2 weeks, shaking daily. When ready, remove the sprigs, and strain out any solids left behind. Bottle and store.

Tahitian Vanilla Rum

3 Tahitian vanilla pods

1 teaspoon raw sugar

1 bottle spiced rum (750 ml)

Vanilla and rum are a natural combination and this infusion serves to enhance some of rum's existing flavors. Not only does rum get some hints of vanilla from aging in wood barrels but vanilla also flourishes in tropical areas around the globe, which are also the areas where rum is typically made.

· · · · ·

Place vanilla pods and sugar into rum and let sit for about 2 weeks. At that point, the vanilla can be removed. If you leave the vanilla in the rum, it will continue to infuse and become more concentrated. Strain out any solids left behind. Bottle and store.

Rooibos Tea-Infused Honey Liqueur

¼ cup rooibos tea leaves

1 bottle Bärenjäger Honey Liqueur

Tea and honey are lovely together—they'll likely make you think of cuddling down under a warm blanket on a chilly fall or winter night. This comforting infusion is a delightful ingredient in the Tea with the Bee Baron cocktail in Chapter 7.

· · · · ·

Place tea leaves in a jar with honey liqueur for 2 days at room temperature. Double strain through cheesecloth. Store in a sealable bottle for up to 2 weeks.

{ Damson Gin }

1 pound fresh damsons
(small plums)

1 pound granulated white
sugar

1 bottle gin (750 ml)

Damson plums became particularly popular in England after being brought to the region by the Romans more than 2,000 years ago. These small, acidic fruits are most often used in jams and preserves; however, they are spectacular when infused into gin, which also has a long history in Great Britain.

· · · · ·

Pit the damsons; then place them with the sugar and gin into a large glass jar. Stir, and then seal the lid. Let sit for 4–6 weeks, shaking every few days. When ready, strain the infused gin into bottles, and save the "drunken damsons." Use the plums as a garnish for cocktails, bake them into a tart, or serve warm in a bowl, topped with vanilla ice cream.

Barrel-Aged Cocktails

When spirits and wine are aged in wooden casks, or barrels, they acquire certain qualities from the wood. Chardonnay wine is often described as "oak-y" after being left in the barrel for a time. Aged sherry, brandy, rum, whiskey, and tequila get a slightly darker hue and deeper flavors from hanging out in wood, as well. Some bartenders have taken to aging mixed cocktails in wood to see what effect it would have. Manhattans, old- fashioneds, Negronis, and Hanky Pankys are a few that have been put into barrels and, a few weeks later, served to the delight of all who tasted them. One suggestion if you try this yourself is to use all-spirit cocktails (meaning no fruits or herbs or other organic materials). Generally, smaller barrels—3 to 5 gallons—work well for this kind of thing. Why not buy a barrel and try it?

{ Black Currant Whisky }

1 pound black currants

1 pound white, granulated sugar (or raw sugar for a more earthy flavor)

1 bottle Scotch (750 ml)

While Scotch remains a favorite among male drinkers, it is often intimidating to women, which is unfortunate because it is a rich spirit with a lot of flavor. This black currant-infused Scotch whisky is a good bridge for female tipplers (cocktail drinkers) who might be otherwise put off by sipping what they think of as their grandfather's drink.

. . . . .

Place all ingredients into a glass jar, and give a good stir. Let sit for 8 weeks, turning the jar to mix the ingredients every 3 days. Strain and bottle.

{ Rose Hip-Infused Organic Vodka }

20 dried rose hips (found in Eastern European and Nordic specialty shops)

1 bottle Square One Organic vodka (750 ml)

This rose hip–infused vodka is a colorful and tasty vodka that works as a very versatile ingredient. Keep a bottle in your home bar and discover the interesting creations you can come up with. The color and flavor make it a versatile ingredient in many cocktails you may create, as you will see in the Eldersour cocktail in this chapter.

. . . . .

Add 20 dried rose hips into the bottle of vodka. Let sit for at least 5 days, agitating once daily. Then strain and set rose hips aside for garnish, returning vodka to its bottle. Rose hips may also remain in the bottle for appeal on the back bar.

{ Cucumber Vodka }

1 cucumber, peeled

1 bottle vodka (750 ml)

If you wished you could take a quick getaway to a high-end spa where they serve cucumber-infused water and rub your aching back, but you just can't get away, a cocktail made with this cucumber-infused vodka may be the next best thing. Wonderful year round, this cucumber-infused vodka is fabulous mixed with homemade lemonade, or muddled with fresh herbs and a squeeze of lime.

· · · · ·

Slice cucumber into spears. Place spears and vodka into a glass jar and let sit for 2 weeks. Shake daily. Double strain and bottle.

{ Chili Oil }

¼ cup red chili powder

1½ cups grape seed oil

Not your typical infusion, this recipe is amazing when several drops are added to a drink. You can also drizzle this oil onto all sorts of culinary dishes but what's good for the kitchen is good for the cocktail glass! See the Oiled-Flaming Mary in Chapter 7 for an idea of how to use it.

. . . . .

Mix the chili powder and grape seed oil. Let sit for a couple of days. Strain through a coffee filter. Bottle the oil and keep for up to a month.

MEAT-INFUSED MIXOLOGY:
The Carnivorous Cocktail

When you think of cocktails, meat may not be the first ingredient that springs to mind. But while bringing a savory element to spirits is something relatively new in modern mixology, the experimentation is catching on worldwide. The unexpected subtle smokiness of bacon or spice of salami will set your drink apart from anyone else's, to say the least! Here are a few ideas and recipes to consider if you choose to explore the carnivorous cocktail.

{ Smoked Bacon-Washed Bourbon }

6–8 strips of ¼ inch–thick
smoked bacon

1 bottle Kentucky bourbon
(750 ml)

If you're one of those meat lovers who declare that "everything's better with bacon," then this infusion is for you. The bacon trend has seen pig fat incorporated into everything from chocolate donuts to candied brittle and why not? In the world of mixology, bacon and bourbon are an obvious choice. Smoked southern barbecue and the South's signature spirit go hand in hand both flavor-wise and geographically. Talk about a southern celebration in a glass!

· · · · ·

1. Cook the bacon until it is no longer raw but not burned. Place the strips of cooked bacon directly into the bourbon bottle, or mix the two in a large glass jar. Let it sit for 2–4 days, giving a little shake daily.

2. Double strain into another large jar, then strain again through cheesecloth. Discard bacon and fat solids. Pour into a sealable bottle. Refrigerate for up to 1 week.

{ Bacon Cherry Creek Cocktail }

2 ounces bacon-washed bourbon (Knob Creek bourbon is a great base)

¾ ounce Cherry-Cinnamon Syrup (Chapter 4)

½ ounce ruby red port

GARNISH: flamed citrus round (Chapter 6) and a strip of cooked bacon (optional)

Bacon and cherries may sound like an odd idea at first but when you think about it, meat and fruit are often used together. Applesauce on pork, Duck á l'Orange, and cranberry relish for turkey are combinations we love, particularly in the United States. So, taking those ideas into account, this cocktail is a winning combination.

· · · · ·

Stir or shake bacon-washed bourbon, syrup, and port with ice, until very cold. Strain into a cocktail glass. Flame orange round over the drink and drop inside. If you want to make a point, serve with a strip of cooked smoked bacon across the rim of the glass.

Prosciutto-Infused Vodka

5–6 strips prosciutto

1 bottle vodka (750 ml)

This Italian dry-cured ham has a light flavor and goes nicely with a relatively neutral spirit such as vodka because it will not overwhelm the meat flavor, as a heavier spirit could. A grape-based vodka could work very nicely with this infusion because it has a lighter, subtly sweeter quality to it than some of the grain vodkas.

· · · · ·

1. Lightly toss the prosciutto in a saucepan on medium heat for only a couple of minutes. Once warmed through, place the prosciutto slices into the bottle of vodka or mix the two in a large glass jar. Let it sit for 2–4 days, giving a little shake daily.

2. Double strain into another large jar, then strain again through cheesecloth. Discard any solids. Pour into a sealable bottle. Refrigerate for up to 1 week.

Prosciutto e Melone

1¾ ounces Prosciutto-Infused Vodka (see recipe in this chapter)

1 ounce fresh cantaloupe juice

¼ ounce maple syrup

½ ounce fresh lemon juice

GARNISH: cantaloupe melon ball wrapped in prosciutto on a wooden skewer

Fresh cantaloupe topped with prosciutto is a common dish in southern Europe where the combination is light enough to act as a tasty first course or be served as a main course with a side salad. The dish inspired this cocktail, which is lovely when sipped on a breezy summer evening.

· · · · ·

Vigorously shake all ingredients except garnish with ice. Strain into a martini glass. Lay skewer across the rim of the glass.

{ Chorizo Mezcal }

1 large or 2 small cooked
spicy chorizo sausages

1 bottle mezcal (750 ml)

In this recipe, the earthy agave and the ethereal smokiness present in mezcal stand up to the savory spice in chorizo sausage. This unique combo is great served straight up as a shot with lime, and sipped alongside a bold, hard white cheese. It is also fun mixed into the Mexican Breakfast cocktail (see recipe in this chapter).

· · · · ·

Place the cooked chorizo directly into the mezcal, or place both into a large glass jar. Let it sit for 2–4 days, giving a little shake daily. Double strain into another large jar, then strain again through cheesecloth. Discard any solids. Pour into a sealable bottle. Refrigerate for up to 1 week.

{ Mexican Breakfast }

2 ounces Chorizo Mezcal

¾ ounce freshly squeezed
orange juice

¼ ounce freshly squeezed
lime juice

½ ounce Bangkok
Lemongrass–Agave Syrup
(Chapter 4)

GARNISH: lime wedge and
Strawberry–Pink Himalayan
Salt Rim (Chapter 6)

This edible cocktail is a spinoff of a margarita, but with obvious twists such as using freshly squeezed orange juice instead of orange liqueur, and of course, the chorizo-infused tequila. While it makes a great brunch cocktail, this unique concoction is delicious any time of the day.

· · · · ·

Rim a rocks glass with Strawberry–Pink Himalayan Salt. Fill with ice, and set aside. Pour all ingredients into a cocktail shaker with ice. Shake well; then strain into ice-filled, rimmed rocks glass. Serve with a lime wedge on the rim of the glass.

{ The Slice }

1 ounce Pepperoni Gin (see recipe in this chapter)

½ ounce yellow Chartreuse liqueur

½ ounce marinara sauce diluted with 2 teaspoons water

¼ ounce organic pineapple juice

¼ ounce lemon juice

6–8 dashes homemade Basil-Thyme Bitters (see recipe in this chapter)

Cheese foam topping (optional)

GARNISH: grilled pepperoni slices; rimmer of toasted pizza crust crumbs and grated parmesan cheese, grilled pineapple and tomato on a skewer

Love pizza? Then this is the cocktail for you! It has pepperoni and marinara sauce, and is topped off by the grated cheese, which is mixed into the grated cheese rimmer.

. . . . .

1. To MAKE THE TOASTED PIZZA CRUST CRUMBS RIMMER: Finely grind ¼ cup pizza crust with 1 tablespoon grated Parmesan cheese in a food processor. Rub the rim of a martini glass with lemon, then dip it into the toasted pizza crust rimmer, and set aside.

2. Pour all liquid ingredients into a cocktail shaker. Shake vigorously with ice, then strain into rimmed glass. Top with cheese foam. Float pepperoni slices on top of cheese foam. Lay skewer across rim of glass.

{ Pepperoni Gin }

1 pound cooked pepperoni

1 bottle gin (750 ml)

Pepperoni Gin is the perfect infusion to create a "pizza in a glass" cocktail as seen in "The Slice" cocktail above.

. . . . .

Place pepperoni and gin in a large glass jar or bowl. Let sit for 2 days in the refrigerator, then move to the freezer until the fat solids collect on the surface of the liquid. Skim off the fats with cheesecloth. Strain, bottle, and store. Refrigerate for up to 1 week.

Dairy and Eggs

Cream and milk have been used in many cocktails and punches over the years, particularly after refrigeration became commonplace. While some vintage recipes using cream date back to the 1930s, some glamorous, creamy potables, such as the grasshopper (vodka or white crème de cacao with green crème de menthe liqueur and cream) and the White Russian (vodka, coffee liqueur and cream), became fashionable in the '50s and '60s. Currently, there is also some experimentation with yogurt, and the Lucas Bols company in Holland even put out a unique yogurt liqueur in 2010. In addition, you also want to take a look at including eggs in your edible cocktails. In both classic and modern mixology, raw egg whites and egg yolks are used. When you're buying your eggs, try to buy market-fresh as hormone-free and free-range chickens produce the healthiest eggs. Note that some of the following recipes call for raw eggs, which may cause salmonella. To avoid salmonella be sure to wash your eggs well in soapy water before breaking them open.

{ Pink Lady }

½ ounce fresh lemon juice

¼ ounce Homemade Grenadine (Chapter 4)

¼ ounce Cherry Heering liqueur

½ ounce cream

1½ ounces dry gin

1 egg white

GARNISH: cherry

The traditional Pink Lady cocktail uses grenadine to give its pink color, but the cherry liqueur added here gives this recipe a tasty twist. In addition, the egg white used here gives this cocktail a silky texture as well as a light, foamy surface. Egg white is popular in many classic recipes as well as many new creations.

. . . . .

Pour all ingredients into a cocktail shaker. Dry shake for 20–30 seconds. Open shaker, add ice, then vigorously shake for another 20–30 seconds. Strain into a cocktail glass and drop the cherry into the drink.

{ Aviation Variation }

¾ ounce lemon juice

¾ ounce maraschino liqueur (Luxardo is a wonderful brand)

1½ ounces gin

1 egg white

½ ounce violet liqueur

The Aviation, a class cocktail, is often considered a gateway cocktail for those who are interested in but not overly acquainted with gin. It gets its name from the sky-blue color that the violet liqueur brings to the glass. Traditionally, this cocktail does not contain egg white, but in this recipe the white fluffy foam on top of the glass is reminiscent of puffy clouds dotting a pale blue sky.

. . . . .

Pour all ingredients except violet liqueur into a cocktail shaker. Dry shake for 20–30 seconds. Add ice, then vigorously shake for another 20–30 seconds. Strain into a martini glass. Gently pour in the violet liqueur, which will settle at the bottom of the glass creating a beautiful layered effect.

{ Ginger Berry Flip }

3 raspberries

¾ ounce Canton Ginger Liqueur

1 ounce Lillet

1½ ounces gin

Dash orange flower water

1 egg yolk

Spicy ginger, rich egg yolk, fresh fruit, and fortified wine are a wonderful flavor combination in this cocktail because the spice balances the sweet and the rich egg and fortified wine give it depth. Warning: It can become addictive.

• • • • •

Put all ingredients into a cocktail shaker and give it a hard dry shake (without ice) for 20–30 seconds. Add ice, then shake vigorously for another 20–30 seconds. Strain into a cocktail glass.

{ Violet Hour }

¾ ounce lemon juice

½ ounce crème de cassis liqueur

½ ounce violet liqueur

½ ounce cream

1½ ounces vodka

1 egg white

Another variation on the Aviation, this cocktail uses vodka to replace the gin and crème de cassis to replace the maraschino liqueur. Floral liqueurs, such as violet liqueur, have been making a comeback recently; they are beautiful both aromatically and aesthetically in vintage-style cocktails.

• • • • •

Dry shake all ingredients for 20–30 seconds. Fill shaker with ice and shake vigorously to chill. Strain into a cocktail glass.

{ Hot Brazilian Passion }

1½ ounces Leblon Cachaça

½ ounce Aperol bitter liqueur

1 ounce Hot Passion Fruit Syrup (Chapter 4)

1 ounce freshly squeezed lemon juice

½ ounce free-range egg white

GARNISH: half a passion fruit

This cocktail is a wonderfully spicy, fragrant twist on the classic sour. If you can find the gorgeous, almost dangerously perfumed passion fruit that hails from the Amazon in this recipe, you may want to try the smaller, sweeter purple passion fruits that have been cultivated in New Zealand and Australia since the 1920s, and have spread around the world, making them a bit easier to find.

• • • • •

Combine all except the garnish in a cocktail shaker and add ice. Shake very hard. Strain into a chilled cocktail glass, and pop a passion fruit half into the drink.

{ Blueberry Yogurtini }

10 ripe blueberries

1 heaping tablespoon yogurt

½ ounce fresh lemon juice

1½ ounces citrus vodka

½ ounce Basic Simple Syrup
(Chapter 4)

This recipe is sure to make you both hungry and thirsty! Most dairy drinks are made with milk or cream, but experimenting with the tangy taste and the thick texture of yogurt makes this cocktail unique!

• • • • •

Muddle the blueberries, yogurt, lemon juice, and simple syrup in the bottom of a mixing glass. Add vodka and ice. Shake vigorously and double strain into a chilled cocktail glass.

{ Devil's Delight }

1 ounce fresh lemon juice

½ ounce Basic Simple Syrup
(Chapter 4)

3 or 4 fresh blackberries

½ ounce Patron XO tequila-
based coffee liqueur

1½ ounces Jim Beam's
Devil's Cut bourbon

1 egg white

6 drops Bitter End Bitter's
Jamaican Jerk Bitters

GARNISH: flamed citrus round
(Chapter 6)

The "angels' share" refers to the amount of alcohol that evaporates while a spirit is aging in a wooden barrel. Jim Beam launched an extra-aged, slightly stronger (it has a higher alcohol percentage) bourbon in 2011 called the Devil's Cut. This cocktail's subtle hints of chocolate, coffee, a little bit of spice make it devilishly delicious!

. . . . .

Pour all ingredients except garnish into a cocktail shaker. Dry shake for 20–30 seconds. Add ice, shake for an additional 20–30 seconds. Double strain into a cocktail glass. Add Flamed Orange Round garnish.

{ Eldersour }

1½ ounces Rose Hip–Infused
Organic Vodka (see recipe in
this chapter)

1 ounce St. Germain
Elderflower Liqueur

1 bar spoon powdered sugar

1 organic, free-range egg
white

½ ounce freshly squeezed
organic lime juice

½ ounce freshly squeezed
organic lemon juice

Dash Peychaud's Bitters

This cocktail has a strong floral influence but also a tart silkiness from the fresh citrus juice and egg white, making it both elegant and accessible to the everyday cocktail lover.

. . . . .

Place all ingredients in the mixing glass and dry shake for 20 seconds. Fill with ice and shake for an additional 20–30 seconds. Strain into a cocktail glass. Garnish with a few additional drops of Peychaud's Bitters.

{ Harvest Hot-Buttered Rum }

1½ ounces spiced rum

¾ ounce apple cider

¼ ounce fresh lemon juice

½ ounce Honey Syrup
(Chapter 4)

3 ounces hot water

GARNISH: 1 teaspoon cinnamon
butter (whip 1 stick of
unsalted butter with ¼ cup
white sugar and 2 teaspoons
of ground cinnamon)

*This warm mixed drink is perfect for the cool nights of autumn. Seasonal apple
cider, spiced rum, and creamy, sweet cinnamon butter make it a delicious way for
you to stay cozy from the inside out.*

. . . . .

Pour all ingredients except for garnish into a heat-resistant bar mug. Top
with pat of butter. Sprinkle with cinnamon.

{ Porto Pirouette }

1½ ounces ruby port

¾ ounce brandy

1 egg yolk

1 teaspoon heavy cream

GARNISH: lemon, white granulated sugar for rim

A flip is a drink that combines sherry, egg yolk, and spirit. This recipe takes this classic cocktail and uses a bright base of ruby port instead of sherry and adds a rich splash of cream. It is a lovely delight any time of day, but is just lovely as an after-diner tipple.

· · · · ·

1. Rub the rim of a cocktail glass with a piece of lemon, and dip it into a plate of sugar to rim the glass. Set aside.

2. Pour all ingredients except garnish into a cocktail shaker, and give it a hard dry shake without ice for 20–30 seconds. Then, open shaker, add ice, and shake again for 20–30 seconds. Strain into the cocktail glass.

{ Tequila Sherry Eggnog }

2 large eggs

3 ounces white granulated sugar

½ teaspoon freshly grated nutmeg

2 ounces añejo tequila

2½ ounces Amontillado sherry

6 ounces whole milk

4 ounces heavy cream

This twist on traditional eggnog uses tequila and sherry instead of rum and brandy. It is a scrumptious alternative if you're looking for new variations of traditional drinks when entertaining over the holidays.

· · · · ·

1. Beat eggs in blender for one minute on medium speed. Slowly add sugar and blend for one additional minute. With blender still running, add nutmeg, tequila, sherry, milk, and cream until combined.

2. Chill thoroughly to allow flavors to combine and serve in chilled punch glasses or champagne coupes, grating additional nutmeg on top immediately before serving.

{ Espresso Brandy Milk Punch }

1 ounce fresh espresso

½ ounce Basic Simple Syrup
(Chapter 4)

½ ounce coffee liqueur

1 ounce half-and-half
(half milk, half cream)

1 ounce brandy

Brandy Milk Punch is a favorite breakfast drink in New Orleans. This version adds a little caffeinated twist by including espresso and coffee liqueur.

• • • • •

Pour all ingredients into a glass, with or without ice, depending on your mood. This can be served warm or cold. Multiply the ratios to make a pitcher for guests.

Homemade Liqueurs

No home or kitchen is complete without a few luscious liqueurs. Typically made with fruits, herbs, nuts, coffee, or cream, these sweet alcoholic treats are lovely sipped on their own as a sort of liquid dessert after a meal, but they are also often delicious when incorporated into simple, classic cocktails like the ones found here.

Making liqueurs is fun and easy—many Italian restaurants, for example, make their own limoncello to serve as an added personal touch at the end of their guests' meals—and homemade liqueurs can incorporate the bounty of your own garden or tasty treasures you come across at the market. They are wonderful personalized presents to give during the holidays and make for thoughtful hostess gifts. Collect decorative bottles to make your homemade liqueurs even more impressive to the recipient. Once bottled, the liqueurs will stay fresh for months, so make plenty and keep several kinds on hand.

Limoncello Della Casa

15–20 lemons, zest only

2 bottles of high-proof vodka (750 ml each)

4 cups white granulated sugar

5 cups water

This delicious and palate-cleansing Italian liqueur is traditionally served chilled and sipped from shot glasses or small liqueur glasses after dinner. It is also sometimes an ingredient in cocktails. Try muddling an ounce of it with fresh rosemary and add gin or vodka for a fresh-tasting libation. Also, try using oranges or grapefruits in place of lemons.

• • • • •

1. Scrub lemons with a vegetable brush so that the skin is very clean. Only choose ripe lemons with no green on them. Lemons with thicker skins are easier to zest because there is less chance of getting too much pith, which can make the limoncello bitter.

2. Place the lemon zest and vodka into a large (one gallon) glass jar with a sealable lid. Let sit for 2–3 weeks in a cool, dark place. The longer it sits, the deeper its color and flavor will be. It is not necessary to shake or stir the mixture.

3. When ready, make a simple syrup by bringing the sugar and water to a boil in a large saucepan, stirring constantly. Lower heat and let simmer for 5 minutes. Let cool and add to lemon zest and vodka mixture. Reseal jar and allow to rest for another 2 weeks. When ready, strain and bottle.

{ Orange-Coffee Liqueur }

1 large, ripe orange

2 cups white granulated sugar

2 cups raw sugar

3 cups water

1½ cups freshly brewed espresso

4 cups vodka

½ cup brandy

1 vanilla bean

This wonderful stand-alone liqueur is also gorgeous when mixed into a dessert-style cocktail, drizzled over ice cream, or mixed with hot coffee on a chilly night. Serve it in a pretty glass with a splash of cream for a luscious late-night treat.

· · · · ·

1. Scrub the orange with a vegetable brush so that the skin is very clean. Then zest the orange, avoiding getting too much pith. Discard (or eat) the rest of the orange. Place all ingredients in a large (one gallon) glass jar with a sealable lid. Let stand one week. (Shake well each day.)

2. Remove the orange peel and let stand two more weeks. Chill and serve.

{ Homemade Irish Cream }

2 cups Irish whiskey

1 can sweetened condensed milk, 14 ounces

1 cup whipping cream

4 eggs

2 tablespoons cocoa powder

2 teaspoons instant coffee

2 teaspoons pure vanilla extract

1 teaspoon almond extract

This liqueur is a tasty treat any time of the year. Served with dessert or as an after-dinner decadence, homemade Irish cream is great to keep chilled in the refrigerator for whenever guests drop by.

· · · · ·

Mix all ingredients in a blender or with a hand held mixer until smooth. Pour into bottles and refrigerate.

{ Advocaat Liqueur }

10 egg yolks

½ teaspoon salt

1½ cups sugar

¼ cup cream

2 teaspoons vanilla extract

1½ cups brandewijn Dutch brandy (or substitute other kinds of brandy)

This lusciously thick and creamy Dutch liqueur originates in Holland and is a great example of the way eggs are used in cocktails. Advocaat is a treat on its own and also a rich ingredient to add to cocktails.

· · · · ·

Beat all ingredients, except brandy, together. Once thick, slowly add brandy while continuing to blend on low speed. When all brandy has been added and mixture is completely combined, slowly heat, whisking constantly. Do not let boil. When mixture is thick enough to coat the back of a spoon, remove from heat and let cool. Bottle and refrigerate.

Bitters

Originally used in health tonics in centuries gone by, bitters—an integral part of a traditional cocktail—are made from alcohol, bark, herbs, and sometimes spices, and today they're often found in health food stores.

Bitters' relationship with cocktails has been described as "salt to a soup." In other words, add too much and the soup is unpalatable. Don't add any, and it will seem as though there is something missing. But when added in the correct amount to an edible cocktail, bitters can provide a boost of flavor and depth of character that elevates a typical drink to a specially crafted imbibing experience. While some bartenders and home chefs are ambitious enough to make their own bitters, today you'll find a myriad of commercial brands available at liquor stores, specialty shops, and online. These are certainly worth exploring and experimenting with! The list of bitters available includes:

○ **ANGOSTURA:** Worldwide, this is the most commonly found bitters. The secret recipe for this concentrated flavoring agent dates back nearly 200 years.

○ **PEYCHAUD'S:** Antoine Amédée Peychaud was an apothecary in New Orleans in the early to mid-1800s. He often served his clients bitters mixed with brandy, sugar, and water. This mix is not only one of the first cocktails on record but the predecessor to today's Sazerac cocktail, popularized in New Orleans.

○ **FEE BROTHERS:** This modern, family-owned business specializes in flavored bitters. Grapefruit, rhubarb, whiskey barrel, mint, Aztec chocolate, and plum are only a few among a myriad of choices.

○ **REGANS' ORANGE BITTERS NO. 6:** Longtime bartender and expert in the industry, Gary Regan has not only written books and trained bartenders around the world, he even came up with his own brand of orange bitters which is used in bars and by mixology devotees everywhere.

○ **BITTER TRUTH:** This multiple award-winning line of bitters has blown the socks off of the bartending industry since its launch in 2006. The company is owned by a couple of German bartenders who have the behind-the-bar experience to recognize what other mixologists may need for tipple tinkering. Among their acclaimed products are the Celery Bitters, Creole Bitters and Jerry Thomas' Own Decanter Bitters. (Jerry Thomas is one of the first bartenders mentioned in history, dating back more than 200 years.)

○ **BITTER END:** Made in Santa Fe, New Mexico, the Bitter End makes small-batch bitters focusing on five world flavors: Jamaican Jerk, Memphis Barbeque, Mexican Mole, Moroccan, and Thai.

- **DR. ADAM ELMEGIRAB:** Based in Scotland, this company makes some fascinating flavors including Dandelion & Burdock, Aphrodite, historic Boker's Bitters, and limited-edition Spanish bitters.

- **BITTERMENS:** This small-batch bitters company is run by a husband and wife team out of Brooklyn, New York. Some of their creative flavors include Tiki, Burlesque, and Orange Cream Citrate, among others.

- **BOB'S BITTERS:** Another artisanal bitters company, Bob's Bitters is based in the United Kingdom and offers interesting flavors such as lavender, licorice, and ginger, among others.

HOMEMADE BITTERS

Many professional bartenders have begun making their own bitters to use at work. If you're a home mixologist you may also like to try your hand at making bitters to "up" your game with homemade ingredients. While mildly labor-intensive, it is worth the extra effort when these flavor boosters bring an extra bang to the drink.

{ *Basil-Thyme Bitters* }

1 cup fresh basil

1 cup fresh thyme

½ cup orange peel

¼ cup lemon pith
(The pith is the white part of the lemon peel. Slice off the outer thick skin, as you would to make a twist. Keep the pith for your bitters.)

½ cup mavi root

½ cup cinchona bark

10 sticks licorice root

⅓ cup grains of paradise (also known as guinea pepper)

Handful of grated or powdered allspice

8 cups (2 liters) high-proof vodka (above 100)

If you are ambitious enough to try your hand at making your own bitters, this herbaceous recipe is a great one. The basil and thyme in these bitters pair wonderfully with gin and vodka, but the combination also goes well with tequila. Most of the unusual-sounding ingredients here can be found at an herb shop or health food store.

• • • • •

Combine all ingredients in a glass jar, and let sit for about 4 weeks. Shake daily. Double strain, bottle, and store in small eyedropper bottles.

BITTER LIQUEURS

While the bitters previously described are concentrated flavor enhancers, and used only a few drops per cocktail, a bitter liqueur is drunk as any other liqueur, wine, or spirit would be: several ounces in a glass, over ice or mixed into a cocktail. They are generally a bit herbal as well, making them wonderful apertifs as their bitterness, rather than sweetness, prepares the palate and digestive system for food. For most Americans—who are typically more accustomed to sweet and salty flavors—bitter can be an acquired taste. Some people think they taste medicinal and scrunch up their faces at the first sip—and they are not entirely wrong—bitters and bitter liqueurs were first used for medicinal purposes. Try them with an open mind, and explore some cocktail recipes calling for bitter liqueurs; the balance and earthiness in the drink will revolutionize the way you think about cocktails. And, the experience will bring you closer to what the original cocktails tasted like over the last two centuries. Worldwide, using bitters and bitter liqueurs is a growing trend in mixology and they are flooding into stores and home bars, making them more accessible than ever.

In this chapter you'll read about some easily found bitter liqueurs, which not only taste wonderful on their own, chilled with a twist of orange or lemon, but also when used in cocktail recipes, both classic and modern. Keep in mind that bitter liqueurs have quite an intense flavor, so if mixed with other ingredients in a drink, these are often used in smaller quantities (generally not more than an ounce).

○ **AMER PICON:** This French bitter liqueur was created by Gaëton Picon in the early 1800s in the south of France around the same time period that the famed French transplant apothecary Antoine Amédée Peychaud was making his now commonly used Peychaud's bitters in New Orleans. Picon syrup is often added to beer or white wine. Amer Picon liqueur has a lovely orange taste and a strong flavor which is nice over ice, if you enjoy bitter liqueur on its own.

○ **AVERNA:** This bitter liqueur is also called *amaro* (which literally means "bitter") and was originally made around 1868. Like all bitters, it is an infusion of spirit with herbs, roots, and notable citrus tones. It is often drunk on its own as a digestif, or after-dinner drink to help one digest a meal.

○ **APEROL:** The recipe for this bitter orange-based liqueur dates back to the early 1900s. Other herbs infused in this elixir include genziana and cinchona. It is interesting to try on its own, mixed with club soda or used in cocktails.

○ **CAMPARI:** This crimson-colored bitter liqueur has strong orange overtones infused with herbs and spices. It is named for its creator, Gaspare Campari, who created the drink for his café in Milan.

○ **CYNAR:** This Italian liqueur features artichoke as one of many herb and plant infusions. It is served before and after meals, and sometimes mixed with juice over ice. It is increasingly common as an ingredient on American cocktail menus.

○ **FERNET BRANCA:** This bitter liqueur is not only used in trendy cocktail bars around the United States now but it has also become a kind of secret handshake of cool imbibers. When someone orders a shot of Fernet in a bar, it can usually be assumed that this person is showing off an evolved palate and knowledge of modern mixology trends. More importantly, however, in small amounts, Fernet's concentrated flavor (it has a sort of herbal, licorice, cough-syrup quality) is a very interesting ingredient to work into cocktail recipes.

○ **GRAN CLASSICO BITTER:** Like many of these bitter liqueurs, the original recipe for this one also dates to the 1800s; this time in Switzerland. Gran Classico Bitter is infused with more than two dozen herbs, among them wormwood, which is most often known for its use in absinthe.

○ **UNDERBERG:** This German bitter was also developed in the 1800s and today is often found in supermarkets and health food stores. Its blend of more than forty herbs makes it a popular digestif. Mixologists have also experimented with it in cocktails.

So feel free to get out there and try some of these bitter liqueurs, even if they seem a bit beyond your comfort zone. After all, cocktails are about creativity and exploration, so get sipping outside the box!

Creative Cocktails

Hopefully this chapter has helped you think outside the proverbial box when it comes to getting creative with cocktails. As you see, the edible cocktail concept incorporates classic mixology but goes a step beyond when it comes to the freedom to experiment. The next chapter goes into the final touch on a drink, which is just as important as the main ingredients. You've come this far, so keep reading to finish off your cocktail with perfection!

Oiled-Flaming Mary
(Chapter 7)

CHAPTER 6

MIXeRs, GaRnisHes, anD iCe

BY THIS POINT IN *EDIBLE COCKTAILS*, YOU HAVE ACQUIRED SOME BASIC MIXOLOGY SKILLS, A BIT OF SPIRIT AND WINE KNOWLEDGE, AND RECIPES FOR homemade ingredients made from homegrown produce and fresh market finds. You've also learned to enhance everyday spirits with infusions, and it is possible that you are looking at dairy and meat in a whole new way. But to truly make your edible cocktail amazing, you need to pay attention to the small details and ensure that your presentation is as perfect as possible. To that end mixers (nonalcoholic beverages mixed into highballs and cocktails), ice, and garnishes are important elements of great drinks, too.

Think about it. Every ingredient in a drink can make or break it and the mixers, ice, and garnishes are just as important as the base spirit because any one of those—from drinkable to aromatic to edible—impact the taste, smell, and presentation of your cocktail. Quality imbibing is a full-sensory experience and this chapter gives you some suggestions on how to make that experience complete.

Mixers

Mixers, the nonalcoholic beverages that you pour into your cocktail, matter as much as the base spirit or wine that you use. A freshly squeezed juice, a good quality carbonated drink, and even the water you add to a straight whiskey can either enhance or destroy your end product. Choose wisely!

JUICES

If you're using juice as a mixer, freshly squeezed is the ideal. Hand squeezing a lime or lemon with a citrus press into each and every individual cocktail may take an extra second or two, but the burst of fresh citrus is worth it. Peeling, cutting, and juicing a pineapple may sound more inconvenient than simply popping open a can but it makes such a difference in the finished cocktail. There is absolutely no comparison. Here are a few juices to keep on hand and a few of the cocktails they will enhance:

Lemon

Freshly squeezed lemon juice is necessary in a myriad of cocktails and brings crisp, refreshing tartness to balance a drink. You can even get creative with lemon juice by trying out unusual types of lemons, such as slightly sweet Meyer lemons, if you can find them at your farmers' market.

Lime

Lime in drinks dates back several centuries to when it was first used by the British navy as a garnish in the gin and tonic. But the gin and tonic wasn't just a refreshing beverage. Instead, the combination had some serious health benefits: The gin was mixed with tonic water, which contains quinine to stave off malaria, and the squeeze of lime was added to protect the sailors from scurvy as they traveled on long voyages.

Orange

Try out different kinds of oranges that may be available seasonally. Blood oranges, for example, are usually available in winter in the United States, and are fabulous to substitute for regular orange juice in all sorts of cocktails. Mandarins, tangelos, and other kinds of orange citrus fruits are also fun to play with in drinks. Freshly squeezed orange juice is always best, of course.

Grapefruit

Grapefruits also come in several varieties so, again, don't be afraid to try out pink ones, yellow ones, and any other hybrid you may come across.

Cranberry

The Cosmopolitan cocktail (vodka, orange liqueur, lime juice, splash of cranberry juice) probably put cranberry juice on the proverbial map when it comes to mixology. However, this tart juice was already used in highballs such as the Madras (vodka, orange juice, cranberry). Try to go with organic pure cranberry juice rather than store-bought cranberry juice cocktails, which contain a lot of other ingredients.

Tomato Juice

You can purée your own red, yellow, or heirloom tomatoes to make delicious and nutritious tomato juice of the highest quality. There is no comparison between home-grown or market-fresh tomatoes and the nearly tasteless ones found in supermarkets, so try to source the best, most flavorful tomatoes when choosing produce to put in your blender.

Tomato Water

Tomato water is a great alternative to tomato juice as it still imparts fresh flavor without the added thickness of puréed tomato juice. Although some people are die-hard Bloody Mary lovers, and therefore like thick tomato juice, tomato water is a great ingredient that can be used in a variety of mixed drinks beyond those that are more traditional.

{ Tomato Water }

8–10 large tomatoes (any garden-picked or farmers' market–fresh varieties will work)

Tomato Water can be preferable to tomato juice because it is not as thick, making it more palatable to some people, and a lighter ingredient to mix in cocktails, as demonstrated in the Caprese Martini in Chapter 7.

• • • • •

1. Place tomatoes in a large bowl. Freeze them overnight.

2. Remove the bowl from the freezer, and leave the tomatoes out to thaw. There will be liquid in the bowl as they return to room temperature and their skins will be loose.

3. Take one tomato at a time, remove its skin, and then squeeze the tomato between your palms over the bowl. (Save the tomato meat for a sauce.) Once finished, double strain the tomato water and store it in a sealable bottle. Freeze any extra for future use.

Lemonade

Homemade lemonade (recipe below) is great for alcoholic and nonal-coholic drinks. You can muddle fresh fruit in the bottom of a glass, fill it with ice, then top it with lemonade for a refreshing drink. If you're looking for a more adult version, add a spirit such as vodka, gin, or tequila, or drizzle in a colorful, fruity liqueur to spike it.

{ Homemade Lemonade }

1 part fresh lemon juice

1 part Basic Simple Syrup or Honey Syrup (Chapter 4)

3 parts water (see Agua Frescas later in this chapter for flavored water ideas)

Enjoy this easy recipe all summer long — with or without a boozy kick. You can also pour this lemonade into ice trays to make delicious and decorative ice cubes for cocktails and punches.

• • • • •

Combine all ingredients in a cocktail shaker, shake well with ice, then strain in a glass-filled Collins glass. Add an ounce of vodka or a drizzle of Limoncello Della Casa (see recipe in Chapter 5) for an adult-friendly kick. Store in the refrigerator up to 5 days.

Melon Juice

When in season, watermelons, cantaloupes, and honeydews are superb in cocktails! Juice them yourself for the freshest taste. Muddle some mint and add a splash of spirit such as rum, vodka, or tequila to make twists on everything from mojitos to margaritas.

Yuzu Juice

The yuzu is a tart and very aromatic citrus fruit from Asia. Its uncommon juice works well with any cocktail into which lemons or limes normally go—and it's delicious when added into Homemade Sweet and Sour Mix (see below).

{ Homemade Sweet and Sour Mix }

2 parts lemon juice

1 part lime juice

½ part yuzu juice
(optional—if you can't find it,
substitute lime juice)

3½ parts Basic Simple Syrup
or Honey Syrup (Chapter 4)

After trying this, you will never, ever buy prebottled sweet and sour mix again! It is so easy to make your own.

. . . . .

Combine all ingredients in a sealable glass container. Stir well and refrigerate for up to 5 days.

Tea

Don't forget about the earthy, garden-fresh aroma and flavor that tea brings to drinks. Whether using it as a mixer in a nonalcoholic cocktail (muddle some fresh fruits, add honey, and top with ice and tea in a tall glass), or as a base for a syrup to use in liquor-filled libations, or as the base for a punch, tea is a versatile ingredient.

AGUA FRESCA

Translating to "fresh water," *agua fresca* is essentially water infused with fresh fruit or veggies or water that is blended with fresh ingredients and strained. Agua fresca is popular in warm-weather countries, but it is easy to make the following recipes or come up with a myriad of combinations with whatever springs from your garden or a jaunt to the local market. Use filtered or purified water, if possible.

{ Cucumber-Lime Water }

1 large cucumber, washed and sliced

½ cup cubed fresh lime

4 cups purified water

If you've been to a spa, you may have sipped cucumber water and thought to yourself, "This is so delicious and easy, why don't I do this at home?" Well, this recipe is the little reminder that every day can feel like an indulgence.

· · · · ·

Combine and allow all ingredients to sit overnight. Strain into a large pitcher. Refrigerate. (Add a few cucumber slices for decoration and further flavor.)

{ Peach-Ginger Agua Fresca }

1 cup sliced, pitted peaches

1 heaping tablespoon
sliced, fresh ginger
(doesn't have to be peeled)

¼ cup Honey Syrup
(Chapter 4)

¼ cup fresh lemon juice

4 cups purified water

This combo has a bit of sweet and a little spice to make it refreshing on its own. Also try adding a splash of whiskey or rum if lounging by a pool on a warm summer day.

. . . . .

Let all ingredients sit together for one hour. Put all ingredients into a blender and pulse until smooth. Strain into a large pitcher. Serve in tall glasses over ice. Garnish with a slice of lemon or candied lemon wheel.

{ Cantaloupe-Mint Agua Fresca }

6 cups peeled, cubed
cantaloupe

10 freshly plucked mint
leaves

½ cup mint Basic Simple
Syrup (Chapter 4)

¼ cup fresh lime juice

4 cups purified water

The sweetness of ripe melons and garden freshness of hand-picked mint are wonderful in this combo because the melon and mint balance each other beautifully. Enjoy!

. . . . .

Let all ingredients sit together for one hour. Put them in a blender and pulse until smooth. Strain into a large pitcher. Serve in a tall glass over ice. Garnish with a slice of lime.

CARBONATED MIXERS

Many traditional highball drinks like Rum and Coke or Gin and Tonic call for carbonated mixers. If you're using them, whenever possible, source out quality ingredients; it's important even for carbonated drinks. Or, if you're feeling adventurous—buy a soda siphon and try making your own carbonated mixers. If you prefer to buy ready-made ones at the store, here are a few above-average brands that you're sure to love.

Soda Water or Club Soda

You may ask yourself how much a specific brand matters in club soda, and the truth is that this is probably the least important carbonated mixer to get uppity about. However, Fever Tree does a lovely line of mixers and their soda water is not an exception.

Tonic

There has been an explosion in the popularity of tonic in recent years, mainly due to the worldwide popularity of gin and tonic. Some great brands include Fever Tree, Q Tonic, and Fentimans.

Ginger Beer

Ginger beer—a nonalcoholic soda—has more spice and bite than ginger ale. Just try it once and you will be hooked! It is specifically called for in drinks such as the Moscow Mule (vodka, lime, ginger beer) and the Dark and Stormy (dark rum such as Gosling's, lime, and ginger beer). Fentimans and Gosling's make excellent ginger beer.

Bitter Lemon

Bitter lemon tends to be more popular in Europe than in the United States, mainly because Europeans are more accustomed to bitter flavors, whereas Americans tend toward the sweet of lemon-lime soda. However, it cannot be stressed enough that bitter lemon is absolutely outstanding in place of the typical sweet lemon-lime soda, or even in place of club soda in all sorts of drinks. Try it with an ounce of Campari in a tall glass over ice on a hot day, and you'll become a convert. Fever Tree makes a great version.

Carbonated Cocktails

How do you get bubbles into your Manhattan, Cosmopolitan, or even glass of wine without adding club soda or champagne? By using a soda siphon, of course. Essentially the curious creativity of bartenders worldwide has sparked this little flurry of carbonating what otherwise would be still drinks. Whether it's necessary or not, it's fun to play. So, if you invest in the tools to make your own carbonated mixers, you may as well toss in a Negroni or a Sazerac and see what happens.

Garnishes

In addition to what you put *in* your drink, you need to keep what you put *on* your drinks in mind, too. After all, part of what makes a cocktail a festive addition to a party or bar menu is the presentation. Garnishes provide an extra burst of flavor, color, and visual whimsy to a drink. The garnish can be sweet, salty, aromatic, or otherwise as long as it adds that little something extra that shows the thought behind the drink and the way it is handed to the guest.

LEMON, LIME, AND ORANGE

Citrus fruits are the most common garnishes, by far. Limes, in particular, are served with cocktails and beer by the truckload on any given week at any given bar! However, there's more than one way to cut a lime.

Half-Quarters

For a half-quarter, cut the lime in half, across the middle. Place the lime cut-side down, and then cut each half into quarters, leaving eight pieces. These cuts are mostly used for highball drinks. For example, someone may traditionally enjoy a lime with their gin and tonic. This type of garnish is typically squeezed into the drink by you, and then dropped into it.

Wedges

To prepare wedges, cut the citrus fruit in half lengthwise (from stem to tail). Place the fruit cut-side down on the cutting board. Cut each half into 3 or 4 long wedges (depending on the size of the fruit). Then make a tiny horizontal slice in the middle of each wedge. This allows you to hang the wedge on the rim of the glass. This cut is perfect if, rather than squeezing the citrus into the drink yourself, you prefer to serve a cocktail with a piece of lime, lemon, or orange on the side of the glass, which allows the guest to squeeze it in.

Wheels

Citrus wheels are a particularly colorful and easy way to spruce up the appearance of a cocktail. Think of a pretty pink "tini" drink with a bright green lime or lemon wheel sitting on its rim. It just screams "I'm having a fancy cocktail," which can make even the least mixology-inclined guest still feel like having this drink is a special experience. To cut wheels, simply place the fruit on the cutting board with the stem and bottom ends pointing toward right and left. Cut those ends off and discard them. Then, slice the fruit all the way along, creating wheels. Then give each wheel a little slit in the peel so that it can be easily placed sitting upright on the rim of a cocktail glass.

Twists

A twist is essentially a sliver of citrus rind. These are most often served with martinis, and most often made with lemons. However, there are no rules as to how you create your own drinks. A lime, orange, or even grapefruit twist can add a little color aroma and flavor to your concoction. The easiest way to make a twist is to cut off the top and tail of a lemon (or other citrus). Then either cut the fruit into wheels, and remove the inner pulp and cut the remaining empty wheel rind into halves. Or another method is to scoop out the inner pulp and then slice the empty fruit rind in half lengthwise, and then slice into strips.

Spirals

Spirals are basically long twists of citrus zest. These are extremely decorative and add a bit of flair and aroma to a cocktail. A spiral can be made several ways: If you are particularly talented with a small cutting knife, or have a spiraling tool, you can simply start at the top of the fruit and move in a circular motion, essentially creating one long strip of fruit zest that then can be cut into a few long pieces. You can also follow the directions for twists, but rather than cutting them in pieces, keep the whole pulp-emptied wheel as one long strip of rind. Twist the piece with your fingers to make it into a spiral, or gently wrap it around a bar spoon to achieve the desired spiral shape.

Flamed Citrus Rounds

Flamed Citrus Rounds are a fun way to get both flavor and a bit of pyro-theatrics into a cocktail. It's fun to watch a guest's face react to a burst of fire over a cocktail. To make this garnish, first, cut a round piece of zest from a citrus fruit. Next, hold it over the finished cocktail in your left hand with the rind facing the drink. Then, gently squeeze the round, rind side out, while simultaneously holding a flame to it (a lighter works best). The natural oils in the rind will squirt out and create a burst of fire as it hits the flame from the lighter. Rub the flamed sphere around the rim of the drink and drop it in.

Playing with Fire!

To make Flaming Spray, just fill a small spray bottle and mix up some high proof spirit (such as Bacardi 151) and a bit of bitters. Spray the mixture into the flame of a lighter over the surface drink, or fruit in the bottom of a glass. Make sure to do this at arm's length from yourself and the guest, as it will spray fire! It looks cool and caramelizes the naturally occurring sugars in the drink and fruit.

RIMMING SUGARS AND SALTS

If you are a margarita lover, you are used to being asked if you would like a salt rim on your glass. If you appreciate the taste that a touch of salt brings to tequila and lime, then by all means, go for it—and get creative with your own salty drink rims. If you are more inclined to skip the salty stuff and lean instead toward sweeter drinks, then you may migrate more toward a sugar-based rimmer for all sorts of cocktails, from spirit-based to sparkling. Either way, here are some suggestions that will work for all sorts of cocktails.

Sweet Rimmers

These sugar-based rimmers incorporate fresh herbs, fruits, and flowers. Try them with cocktails and desserts—and, feel free to adjust the ratios of ingredients to suit your taste buds.

{ Lavender Sugar Rim }

2 heaping tablespoons of dried lavender buds (Some health, herb, or tea shops may carry dried lavender flowers. You can also buy fresh lavender at many farmers' markets: Remove the flowers, and dry them yourself on a baking sheet.)

1 cup white granulated sugar

This upscale lavender sugar not only makes for a delicious rim on a cocktail but you also can sprinkle it on desserts, fresh fruit, or cakes.

· · · · ·

Place lavender buds and ¼ cup of sugar into a food processor and grind until blended and powdery. Mix with remaining sugar and store in an airtight container.

{ Meyer Lemon Rimming Sugar }

3 heaping tablespoons
Meyer lemon zest

1 cup white granulated
sugar

The sweet and tart taste of Meyer lemons is delicious whether you're using them to flavor foods or drinks. This rimmer is lovely on a Lemon Drop cocktail, a glass of nonalcoholic lemonade, or when sprinkled on cupcakes and ice cream.

· · · · ·

1. Zest a Meyer lemon, removing as little pith as possible. Dry the zest overnight.

2. Then, place the lemon zest and ¼ cup of sugar in a food processor and grind until well-mixed and powdery. Mix with remaining sugar and store in an airtight container.

{ Mint Rimmer }

3 tablespoons dried mint

1 cup raw sugar

There are many ways to make mojitos, and this rimmer not only looks amazing on the rim of the glass, you can also use the ingredients in the cocktail itself when you muddle the fresh mint and sugar. Don't forget to use this rimmer on the glass of cocktails featuring ingredients such as watermelon juice or mango purée; its addition makes for delicious, refreshing combinations!

· · · · ·

Place the mint and ¼ cup raw sugar into a food processor and grind until well mixed and powdery. Mix with remaining sugar and store in an airtight container.

Salty Rimmers

Salt-based rimmers are great for well-known drinks such as margaritas or salty dogs, for which plain salt (usually kosher salt) is typically used. If you're serving a drink with a salty rim, consider using these rimmers on only half the glass. This way your guest has the option of enjoying the cocktail with or without the salt.

{ Chili Salt Rim }

2 heaping tablespoons red chili flakes

1 heaping tablespoon red chili powder

1 heaping tablespoon dried lime zest

½ cup kosher salt

In the Southwestern United States, chili is a staple in most food dishes and it's becoming increasingly popular in cocktails. A pinch of this chili rimmer is amazing when tossed into the cocktail shaker and mixed directly with the drink. It can also be used as a condiment for cooking meats, pastas, and other dishes that benefit from a bit of spicy zing.

• • • • •

Place red chili flakes, chili powder, dried lime zest, and ¼ cup kosher salt into a food processor, and grind until well blended and slightly powdery. Mix with remaining kosher salt and store in an airtight container.

{ Strawberry-Pink Himalayan Salt Rim }

3 heaping tablespoons of
dried strawberries
(Buy dried strawberries at a
gourmet grocer or make your
own by slicing garden-fresh
strawberries and allowing
them to dry on a baking sheet
for a couple of days.)

1 cup pink Himalayan salt

Pink Himalayan salt is known for its high mineral content, particularly iron. Mixed with dried strawberries, this sweet and salty rimmer is amazing for strawberry cocktails, and is also interesting sprinkled on poultry such as a lemon-roasted chicken or orange duck.

· · · · ·

Place the dried strawberries and ¼ cup salt into a food processor and grind until blended well and slightly powdery. Mix with remaining salt and store in an airtight container.

{ Salty Dog Rimmer }

2 heaping bar spoons of
dried grapefruit zest
(peel grapefruit zest and cut
it into strips, then allow it to
dry on a baking sheet)

1 cup kosher salt

The Salty Dog is essentially a Greyhound (one ounce of gin or vodka and grape-fruit juice in a tall glass) with a salt rim. Make the rim more interesting by incorporating some actual grapefruit zest into it. This grapefruit salt mixture is also interesting used in poultry and pork dishes.

• • • • •

Place the grapefruit zest and ¼ cup of kosher salt in a food processor and grind until well mixed and powdery. Mix with remaining salt and store in an airtight container.

OTHER GREAT GARNISH IDEAS

Garnishes are a great place to get creative with ingredients that bring something special to a drink. Beyond citrus garnishes and rimmers, there are a few other outside-the-box ideas.

{ Quick-Pickled Grapes }

½ cup champagne vinegar (found in supermarkets or gourmet shops)

½ cup water

3 tablespoons white, granulated sugar

1 tablespoon kosher salt

1 teaspoon juniper berries

1 teaspoon pink peppercorns

1 teaspoon yellow mustard seeds

1 teaspoon dried dill

1 teaspoon dried herbes de Provence

1 cup green grapes

These Quick-Pickled Grapes appear in the Duchess cocktail (see recipe in Chapter 3). They are easy to make, and add an impressive culinary—and edible—presentation to your drink.

· · · · ·

1. Combine vinegar, water, sugar, salt, herbs, and spices in a small saucepan over low heat. Stir until sugar and salt dissolve and the mixture just comes to a simmer. Take off the heat and let cool to lukewarm.

2. Pour pickling liquid over the grapes in a container and ensure that the grapes are completely covered by the liquid. Allow to fully cool and then cover and place in the refrigerator.

3. Your grapes will be perfectly pickled once they have had a chance to soak overnight. They will last up to 1 week in the refrigerator.

{ Candied Limes }

2 large or 3 small limes

1 cup white, granulated sugar

2 tablespoons sugar

1 cup water

Limes are probably the most common garnish for cocktails, but that doesn't mean you can't play with the way they're presented. This versatile recipe is applicable for lemons, oranges, grapefruits, ginger, and pretty much any other fruit with which you want to experiment. You'll find these limes in several cocktail recipes throughout the book.

· · · · ·

1. Slice limes into thin rounds. Blanch in a pot of boiling water for 2 minutes and drain. Set limes aside on cooling rack.

2. In the same pot, combine water and 1 cup sugar. Bring to a simmer and add lime slices. Simmer for 10–15 minutes, until the white pith of the limes looks translucent (may take longer if pith is especially thick or dense). Drain and spread out on a cooling rack to dry for at least 1 hour.

3. Next, put 2 tablespoons of sugar in shallow bowl or saucer. When limes are dry, coat both sides of the lime slices by pressing them into the sugar (you may need more sugar for good coverage). Store in an airtight container and layer between parchment paper or plastic wrap till ready to use. (Store in the freezer if this recipe yields more than you can use in 2–3 days.)

{ Candied Lavender Sprigs }

12 lavender stems, leaves removed

½ cup Lavender-Rosemary Syrup (Chapter 4)

¼ cup Lavender Sugar Rim (see recipe in this chapter)

¼ cup Meyer Lemon Rimming Sugar (see recipe in this chapter)

These lavender sprigs are gorgeous when draped over the rim of a cocktail glass, dipped into a drink as an extra bit of fanciful flavor, or when used as garnish on a dessert plate.

· · · · ·

With a pastry brush, gently coat each lavender stem with lavender syrup, then roll it into a mixture of Lavender Sugar Rim and Meyer Lemon Rimming Sugar. Let dry on wax paper for a couple of hours.

{ Blue Cheese-Stuffed Chili Olives }

2½ pounds pitted, green olives

3 cups water

2 tablespoons kosher salt

1 lemon, washed and cut into wedges

3 fresh basil leaves

1 tablespoon chopped, fresh oregano

1 tablespoon red chili powder

1 cup white wine vinegar

3 cloves garlic

½ cup olive oil

Softened blue cheese

Prepare these olives yourself to nibble alongside apéritifs before dinner or to use as a garnish in a "dirty" martini.

· · · · ·

1. Soak green olives in enough water to cover them for a week, changing water each day. On the eighth day, bring 3 cups water and the salt to a boil. Add to the olives and the water in which they have been soaking, the lemons, fresh herbs, chili powder, vinegar, garlic, and olive oil. Simmer on low for 5 minutes.

2. Remove from heat, let cool, and store in the refrigerator for up to a month. Stuff the olives with blue cheese when you are ready to serve.

Ice

Ice has been a hot topic among mixologists over the last few years. The shape, density, and size of the ice used in cocktails is especially important. Denser, larger ice tends to be more effective in cooling cocktails without watering them down the way smaller, hollow, mass-produced ice does. Even though some necessary dilution comes by way of shaking liquor with ice in a cocktail shaker, using an ice ball (a ball of ice roughly the size of a tennis ball) or more solid ice cubes allows for slower dilution in a glass. This slower dilution is particularly important when serving a guest a Scotch on the rocks, for example, because one large chunk of ice will allow enough water to seep slowly into the spirit to "open" the flavor as well as cool it, without making a fine whiskey too watery, too fast.

One interesting idea bartenders and at-home entertainers can do to use that dilution to their advantage is to make flavored ice. Ice cubes made of tonic can only make a gin and tonic better because the melting tonic water cools and boosts flavor as it melts. Using fresh juices and other beverages to make ice cubes will have the same flavoring effect, and is a good way to bring more market-fresh fruit into your drink, year round. However, keep in mind that pure liquor doesn't freeze, so if you want to play with adding spirits to your specialty ice, do so in very small amounts.

Adding ice to your cocktail can also add a decorative element to the drink if those cubes are full of edible flowers, berries, or chunks of fruit. Here are some ice recipes that are sure to heat up your cocktail!

{ Peychaud's Bitter Ball }

1 ice-ball mold (Some models
are single balls, and others
make 3 or more ice balls.)

Peychaud's Bitters

Filtered water

*This ice ball flavored with Peychaud's Bitters is used to cool and flavor the
Sazerac on the Rock cocktail found in Chapter 7. Ice balls are gaining popularity
in bars and at home. Increasingly, you can find ice-ball molds online as well as in
some specialty cooking and bar-product stores.*

· · · · ·

Fill the mold with filtered water; then add eight dashes of Peychaud's
Bitters per ice ball. Freeze until needed.

{ Blueberry-Lemonade Ice Cubes }

½ cup blueberries

1 cup lemonade

*For both alcoholic and nonalcoholic drinks, blueberries and lemons work well
together. If you are having a party where colorful, edible ice will make an impres-
sion, these cubes are easy to make ahead of time. As these melt, they impart
flavor into the glass, so feel free to switch other berries in place of the blueberries and other juices instead of lemonade so that the colors and tastes enhance
whichever drink or punch you are serving.*

· · · · ·

Place a couple of blueberries into each opening in an ice cube tray. Fill with
lemonade. Freeze until needed.

{ Holiday Ice Wreath }

1 bundt cake pan

2 cups cranberry juice

½ cup water

¼ cup Basic Simple Syrup
(Chapter 4)

1 lemon sliced into wheels

The holidays are full of entertaining and any extra touches relating to food and drink presentation go a long way to impress guests. This holiday ice wreath both cools a punch and continues to add flavor to it as the ice melts.

. . . . .

Fill the bundt cake pan with all ingredients, spacing the lemon wheels around the pan. Freeze and use when needed.

A Decorative Touch

Congratulations! You have covered all sorts of approaches to creating the edible cocktail. Now you are probably excited to get cooking and shaking, growing and stirring. The next chapter features many cocktail recipes that you will enjoy making. It will also serve as a springboard for your own twists and cocktail creations that use the garden and kitchen for inspiration.

CHAPTER 7

MORe cocktail Recipes!

NOW THAT YOU KNOW HOW TO GROW AND MAKE YOUR OWN INGREDIENTS FROM SCRATCH, AND CAN IMPRESS EVEN THE MOST DIE-HARD COCKTAIL SNOBS by including some upscale ice (and maybe even a slab of bacon) in their drinks, you are ready to shake, swizzle, and roll. You've seen recipes for various cocktails scattered throughout this book, but here you'll find even more drink recipes—and some bonus bartending and entertaining tips—with the hopes that you will be cooking, mixing, and shaking for a long time to come. Pat yourself on the back, raise a glass, and toast to a fun, culinary approach to the alchemy of mixology. Cheers!

Herby Concoctions

This grouping of cocktail recipes is meant to help you pluck inspiration from your own cocktail garden. Fresh herbs bring aroma, taste, color, and uniqueness to cocktails. They can be muddled, cooked into syrups or preserves, infused directly into spirits, used as garnishes, or even set afire and tossed into the shaker to add a smoky quality to the drink. The drinks you'll see in this section are delicious guidelines for you to start thinking about coming up with your own herbal concoctions with whatever is seasonal in your area, any time of the year.

{ Summer Sage }

2 sage leaves

1 bar spoon sugar

1½ ounces vodka

¾ ounce Limoncello Della Casa (Chapter 5)

1½ ounces fresh grapefruit juice

Dash orange bitters

This aromatic cocktail mingles fresh sage with sweet lemon and tangy grapefruit, creating a balanced rainbow of flavors—and a pleasurable experience for the senses.

· · · · ·

1. Muddle 1 sage leaf with sugar in the bottom of a mixing glass. Add liquid ingredients. Shake vigorously with ice. Double strain into a martini glass to hold back bits of sage.

2. Garnish with the remaining whole sage leaf. Give it a slap on the palm of your hand to release the oils, flavor, and aroma, then place it on the rim of the glass, just floating on the drink's surface.

{ Rose-Mary-Me }

¾ ounce lime juice

½ ounce agave syrup

¾ ounce reposado tequila

1½ ounces Rosemary-
Infused Reposado Tequila
(Chapter 5)

GARNISH: salt rim and lime
wedge

The herbaceous quality of rosemary works extremely well with aromatic spirits such as gin and tequila. This recipe could be called a rosemary margarita, except a margarita normally includes orange liqueur. It's a great example of getting creative with a classic drink recipe and giving it your own garden-to-glass twist by using your own infused spirit.

· · · · ·

Rim the glass with salt; set aside. Pour all ingredients into a cocktail shaker with ice. Shake vigorously and strain into glass. Place lime wedge on rim of glass.

{ Minty Vodka Mojito }

½ lime, cut into wedges

5 leaves fresh mint

¾ ounce Mint Syrup
(Chapter 4)

2 ounces vodka

Splash bitter lemon soda

Mojitos are typically made with rum, lime, mint, and sugar, and are sometimes topped with a splash of club soda. This drink is a vodka version of a mojito, and in a great warm-weather alternative, as it makes for a refreshing drink.

• • • • •

Muddle lime, mint leaves, and Mint Syrup in a cocktail shaker. Add vodka. Shake vigorously. Strain into an ice-filled tall glass. Top with a splash of bitter lemon soda.

{ Sage and Pine Martini }

½ ounce Smoked-Sage Syrup
(Chapter 4)

¼ ounce fresh lemon juice

2 ounces Pine-Infused Gin
(Chapter 5)

½ ounce dry vermouth

GARNISH: lemon twist

The fresh smell of pine and smoked sage found in this recipe are a unique combination. The mingled woodsy, outdoor aromas and flavors of these ingredients make sipping this drink feel like a wander through the mountains.

• • • • •

Shake all ingredients except garnish with ice. Strain into chilled martini glass. Garnish with a lemon twist.

{ Cilantro-Cucumber Vodka Collins }

3 sprigs cilantro

2 slices cucumber

½ ounce lemon

½ ounce Basic Simple Syrup
(Chapter 4)

1¾ ounces Cucumber Vodka
(Chapter 5)

Top with club soda

Fresh cilantro and cucumber-infused vodka bring market-fresh (or your own garden-fresh) aromas and flavors to this refreshing twist on a classic vodka collins.

· · · · ·

Muddle 2 sprigs of cilantro, the cucumber, lemon, and Basic Simple Syrup in the bottom of a cocktail shaker. Add Cucumber Vodka. Shake with ice, then strain into collins glass over fresh ice. Top with club soda. Garnish with remaining cilantro sprig.

{ Lavender Gin Sour }

¾ part fresh lemon juice

¾ part homemade Lavender-Rosemary Syrup (Chapter 4)

1¾ parts gin

GARNISH: Lavender Sugar Rim (Chapter 6)

This simple sour drink follows the classic sour recipe of 2 parts spirit to 1 part each citrus and sweet. The sweet lavender, tart lemon, and aromatic gin complement each other beautifully on your nose and tongue. Try your own substitutions to come up with your own sours.

. . . . .

Rim half a martini glass with Lavender Sugar, then set aside. Vigorously shake lemon juice, Lavender Syrup, and gin with ice; then strain into rimmed glass.

{ Lavender-Minted Tea }

4 ounces brewed mint tea

1 ounce lavender-infused vodka (follow infusing guidelines in Chapter 5)

½ ounce Basic Simple Syrup (Chapter 4)

GARNISH: Candied Lavender Sprig (Chapter 6)

This tea-based drink can be served hot or cold—like the tea itself—and you can leave out the alcohol if you want to make a virgin version for designated drivers or underage guests.

. . . . .

Pour mint tea, vodka, and Simple Syrup into a cocktail shaker. Shake with ice and strain into a cocktail glass. Garnish with Candied Lavender Sprig. For hot version, heat all ingredients, except vodka, and pour into a teacup or bar mug. Add the vodka last, and give it a stir before serving.

{ Peachy Basil-Tini }

5 fresh basil leaves

¼ ounce Basic Simple Syrup
(Chapter 4)

¾ ounce Peach Purée
(Chapter 4)

¼ ounce fresh lemon juice

1½ ounces citrus vodka

Peach and basil are a great combination in both food and drinks when the sweetness of a fresh, ripe peach bounces off the aroma of sweet, earthy, freshly picked basil. This drink is beautiful for a summer party and even works as a festive holiday drink if you made peach purée when peaches were in season and saved some in your freezer!

• • • • •

Muddle 4 leaves of the basil, peach purée, Simple Syrup, and lemon juice in the bottom of a cocktail shaker. Add vodka and ice. Shake vigorously and double strain into a martini glass. Garnish with a basil leaf on the rim of the glass.

{ Ginger Sun }

1 inch slice of fresh ginger

½ ounce freshly squeezed lemon juice

¾ ounce Hibiscus-Cabernet Syrup (Chapter 4)

1 ounce pomegranate juice

1½ ounces citrusy gin or vodka

1 lemon wheel (for garnish)

Fresh ginger can be amazing in cocktails. This versatile spice is fresh and spicy at the same time and it lends this flavor profile to your drink. This cocktail combines the tastes of sweet and spice with layers of flavor from the rich cabernet wine–based syrup.

. . . . .

Muddle fresh ginger in the bottom of a mixing glass with lemon juice. Add Hibiscus-Cabernet Syrup, pomegranate juice, and gin. Shake with ice. Strain into a martini glass. Garnish with a lemon wheel on the rim of the glass.

Preserves, Jam, Marmalade, and Custard in Cocktails

In Chapter 4, you learned many reasons why fruit preserves are great for cocktails: not only do they give a burst of seasonal, garden-fresh flavor any time of the year but they also add sweetness and texture to a cocktail. Here are a few examples of their use in drinks. Use these as guidelines to make your own!

{ Bellini 75 }

1 sugar cube

Dash Fee Brothers
Rhubarb Bitters

1 ounce gin

½ ounce Peach Purée
(Chapter 4)

3 ounces sparkling wine

As with the Italian 75 in Chapter 3, this is another elegant combination of ingredients from two classic champagne cocktails, a Bellini and a French 75. The fruity peach purée integral to a Bellini is lovely with gin, and you could also substitute peach-friendly brandy for gin in this cocktail for a richer flavor, as is sometimes done in a classic French 75.

· · · · ·

Muddle the sugar cube and rhubarb bitters in the bottom of a mixing glass. Add gin, Peach Purée, and ice. Shake well, then strain into a chilled champagne flute. Top with ice-cold sparkling wine.

{ The Whiskied Fig }

1 heaping bar spoon Fig and Whiskey Preserve (Chapter 4)

½ ounce fresh lemon juice

2 ounces bourbon

½ ounce St. Germain Elderflower Liqueur

GARNISH: lemon twist (Chapter 6)

Figs are rich and dense in texture and flavor, and therefore stand up to the richness in dark spirits such as rum, brandy, and whiskey. Once you've cooked up some homemade Fig and Whiskey Preserve (see recipe in Chapter 4) and enjoyed it as an edible ingredient with cheese and bread, shake it into this luscious drink.

· · · · ·

Muddle the Fig and Whiskey Preserve with lemon juice. Add bourbon and liqueur. Shake all ingredients vigorously with ice. Double strain into a chilled cocktail glass. Garnish with a lemon twist.

{ Temptation Gage }

4 pineapple sage leaves plus 1 for garnish

Dash Basic Simple Syrup (Chapter 4)

Dash lemon juice

1¾ ounces Hendricks Gin

⅓ ounce Lillet Blanc

1 bar spoon Lemon and Mandarin Curd (Chapter 4)

This drink incorporates cucumber and rose-flavored gin with fortified wine, Lemon and Mandarin Curd to create a hybrid drink with herbal notes and a silky texture. Its balanced flavor and varied ingredients make this drink a great example of an edible cocktail.

· · · · ·

Muddle 4 pineapple sage leaves with sugar syrup and lemon juice in the bottom of a cocktail shaker. Add all other ingredients and ice. Shake vigorously and strain into a chilled cocktail glass. Garnish with a pineapple sage leaf.

{ Brazilian Breakfast }

1½ ounces Leblon Cachaça

½ ounce Cointreau orange liqueur

½ ounce Basic Simple Syrup (Chapter 4)

1 ounce freshly squeezed lemon juice

2 bar spoons Lime Marmalade (Chapter 4)

½ ounce free-range egg white (optional)

GARNISH: lime zest

This cocktail is an homage to the famed gin-and-orange marmalade Breakfast Martini popularized in London, where it was created by famous Italian barman Salvatore Calabrese, a forerunner in the trend of using jam in cocktails. Marmalade, often served on crumpets with tea for breakfast in England, is a highlighted ingredient in that drink, hence the name. This Brazilian twist suggests a homemade lime marmalade (limes grow well in Brazil) and cachaça (Brazilian sugarcane rum), and includes an egg white option for luscious texture. Finish by grating a little lime zest on the surface of the drink for a really aromatic note.

· · · · ·

Combine all except garnish and egg white in a cocktail shaker, and stir quickly to mix the marmalade. Add egg white, if using, and then add ice. Shake very hard, and fine-strain into a chilled cocktail glass. Finish with grated lime zest.

Green Drinks: Cocktails with an Eye Toward Sustainability

If you're into edible cocktails, there's a good chance that you're a proponent of eating and drinking "green" whenever possible. In other words, by paying attention to sustainability when you shop for seasonal, local foods for your meals and cocktails, you are bringing a "green" philosophy to your nibbling and tippling, as well. Here are a few recipes featuring organic and sustainable spirits, made by companies who use organic grains or fruits as the source for their spirits, and distill them in the most environmentally friendly way possible. There are many more of these spirits coming onto market shelves so keep an eye out for them!

{ Flor de Jamaica }

1½ ounces Don Q Gold Rum

½ ounce fresh lemon juice

¾ ounce Hibiscus Syrup (Chapter 4)

1 dash orange bitters

GARNISH: hibiscus flower (optional) and lemon twist

Don Q rum has been celebrated for its consciousness with regard to the environment. While the liquor industry, like all big business, can be careless with this aspect of production, the companies who do concentrate on disposing of waste responsibly, as well as promoting an earth-friendly message, are highly appreciated by eco-conscious cocktail lovers.

· · · · ·

Pour all ingredients except garnish into a cocktail shaker with ice. Shake, strain into a cocktail glass. Garnish with lemon twist and hibiscus flower.

{ Watermelon Margarita }

½ ounce fresh lime juice

½ ounce agave syrup

¼ ounce organic Loft
Tangerine Cello liqueur

1 ounce fresh organic
watermelon juice

1½ ounces organic tequila
(silver or reposado)

GARNISH: Mint Rimmer
(Chapter 6)

Everybody loves a refreshing, ice-filled glass of fresh lime juice and tequila on a hot day. Because of the watermelon juice in this recipe, this cocktail is ideal for a steamy, summer barbecue when you may already be buying watermelon for your picnic. And, if you are able to get hold of organic fruits, it is easy to make this drink eco-friendly.

• • • • •

Rim a rocks glass with Mint Rimmer. Set aside. Pour all ingredients into a cocktail shaker with ice. Strain into glass.

{ Spiced Margarita Mezcaltini }

1 slice jalapeño

½ ounce freshly squeezed lime juice

½ ounce agave nectar

¾ ounce freshly squeezed grapefruit juice

1½ ounces Del Maguey Mezcal (organic)

GARNISH: Chili Salt Rim (Chapter 6)

Although most tequilas are organic by nature (there isn't a lot of pesticide spraying onto agave plants), there are some marketed specifically as organic. Mezcal (which can most simply be referred to as a smoky cousin of tequila) is made from roasted, pressed agave hearts. Adding a bit of spice to this cocktail recipe is a natural concept considering that Mexican food is quite spicy so this drink complements the cuisine of Mezcal's native country.

· · · · ·

1. Rim half a martini glass with chili salt. Set aside.

2. Muddle jalapeño, lime juice, and agave nectar in the bottom of a mixing glass. Add grapefruit juice and mezcal. Shake well and gently strain into glass.

{ Detox Me Martini }

½ ounce lime juice

½ ounce Ginger Honey Syrup
(Chapter 4)

1½ ounces organic gin

¾ ounce VeeV Açai Spirit

1 ounce pomegranate juice

GARNISH: pinch freshly grated
ginger

Pomegranate juice and açai berries are said to have antioxidant qualities, which means that they are loaded with vitamins and even block harmful free radicals in the body. So, mixing organic gin, pomegranate juice, and VeeV Açai Spirit into this cocktail can almost make you feel as though you're sipping a health tonic!

· · · · ·

Shake all ingredients (except garnish) with ice. Strain into a chilled martini glass. Sprinkle freshly grated ginger over the surface of the drink.

{ Basil Grass Lemon Drop }

5 fresh basil leaves

1 inch piece of fresh
lemongrass

¼ part Simple Syrup

½ part fresh lemon juice

1 part Limoncello Della Casa
(Chapter 5)

1½ parts Square One Basil
Vodka

GARNISH: lemon wheel
(Chapter 6)

Fresh herbs from your garden and an organic spirit make this drink an ideal way to stay eco-friendly while indulging in an alcoholic libation. Not only are you supporting greener businesses, but you can clink glasses to being earth-friendly while doing it.

· · · · ·

Muddle basil, lemongrass, Simple Syrup, and lemon juice in a mixing glass. Add Limoncello and Square One Basil Vodka. Shake well with ice. Double strain into a chilled cocktail glass. Garnish with a lemon wheel.

Greening Your Bar

If you own a bar and want to make it more earth friendly, or if you're looking to make your home a little more "green," it's important that you realize that being eco-friendly goes beyond organic cocktails. H. Joseph Ehrmann, the proprietor of San Francisco's eco-friendly saloon Elixir, suggests that you consider the following points:

- *Where is your plumbing leaking or dripping? This wastes an incredible amount of water.*

- *Are there flow control devices on your faucets to conserve water?*

- *Are your refrigeration devices operating efficiently? Are the filters clean and the seals intact?*

- *Are you using appropriate compact fluorescent lighting to reduce energy consumption?*

- *Does your local waste management allow you to break down waste into landfill, compost, and recycling, and are you doing it?*

- *Are you making things like simple syrup and fresh juices, which not only provide better drinks, but reduce packaging waste?*

- *Can you source something locally that was previously imported or shipped cross-country, reducing the supply chain's carbon footprint?*

{ Golden Gate }

2 ounces Square One
Organic Vodka

2 ounces Persimmon Purée
(Chapter 4)

This cocktail uses seasonal persimmons and traditional holiday spices, which give this drink its decidedly light and modern taste. The homemade Persimmon Purée, which utilizes seasonal ingredients, is a gorgeous complement to a quality, certified organic spirit.

· · · · ·

Place vodka and purée in a shaker with lots of crushed ice. Shake vigorously for 30 seconds. (This cocktail needs dilution or it will be too thick, so shake away!) Strain into chilled martini glass. No garnish required as the vanilla bean specks from the Persimmon Purée float beautifully in the glass.

Make It Mindful

Gary Regan, a mixologist and educator, encourages bartenders to create a richer experience for their guests by not only focusing on quality cocktails, but also personal interaction, believing that the "mindful bartender" pays equal attention to guests and to staff. Regan says, "It's good to understand that in many cases, dishwashers, kitchen porters, and people whose hourly rate is minimal at best, are pretty much invisible while they are at work. They are taken for granted, and few people give them the time of day. Mindful bartenders who make an effort to communicate mindfully with these people are usually rewarded immediately with a look that tells them, 'thanks for taking 30 seconds to talk to me, everyone else ignores me.'" If someone is helping you out at a party, practice mindful bartending to show them your appreciation too. Whether you work in a bar or are hiring help for your home party, practice mindfulness and express your appreciation. Good drinks become great when served with positive energy!

More Fun Drinks!

Creativity is key when making cocktails. Whether wine- or spirit-based, aromatic or fruity, classic or experimental, the main idea is to have fun trying new flavor combinations while mixing a drink that is balanced on the palate—not too sweet, not too tart, not too bitter, and so on. One rule of thumb is to follow a classic cocktail recipe, then give it your own flair. Hopefully the drinks in this section will give you even more ideas of ways to get shaking!

{ Oiled-Flaming Mary }

1 apricot, pitted and halved

½ ounce fresh lemon juice

½ ounce Basic Simple Syrup (Chapter 4)

1½ ounces gin

2 dashes bitters (Get creative and use flavored bitters if you want!)

1 sprig rosemary

6 drops Chili Oil (Chapter 5)

This recipe pulls its inspiration from a variety of food ingredients and cocktails to create a crazy concoction of gin, chili-infused oil, apricot, and rosemary. But this cocktail really comes to the forefront as a showstopper when you light it on fire before serving. It's sure to turn heads—and impress your guests!

· · · · ·

1. Muddle the apricot with lemon juice and Basic Simple Syrup in the bottom of a mixing glass. Add gin and bitters and set aside.

2. Set the rosemary on fire and collect the smoke in an upside down cocktail tin. Throw the burned rosemary into the drink.

3. Add ice, shake well, and double strain into a cocktail glass. Garnish with 6 drops of Chili Oil on the surface of the drink.

{ Blame It on Rio }

2 ounces Leblon Cachaça

1 ounce freshly squeezed lime juice

1 ounce Jalapeño Syrup (Chapter 4)

2 slices of cucumber, peeled

1 small pinch of sea salt

GARNISH: cucumber slice or jalapeño slice

This delicious drink combines tastes of spice, sour, bitter, and sweet. It also has a tiny hint of salt, which means that this cocktail pleases all the parts of the palate. It's particularly wonderful in hot weather, as chili actually has a cooling effect on the body, even if the opposite seems true.

. . . . .

Combine all the ingredients except garnish in a cocktail shaker, and add ice. Shake vigorously, and then strain into a rocks glass filled with ice. Garnish with a cucumber slice, or a jalapeño slice for the daring.

{ The Mario }

¾ ounce tangerine juice

1 ounce Plymouth gin

½ ounce dry vermouth

¼ ounce Homemade Grenadine (Chapter 4)

¼ ounce Combier liqueur

3 drops Chili Oil (Chapter 5)

GARNISH: lime twist

This drink has a bit of a chili kick after you experience the initial sweetness from the grenadine, which makes for an interesting cocktail-sipping experience. Having variety and layers in flavor brings uniqueness to cocktails, something all guests can appreciate.

. . . . .

Combine all ingredients except garnish in a cocktail shaker. Add ice, shake well. Strain into a chilled cocktail glass and garnish with a lime twist.

{ Caprese Martini }

5 fresh basil leaves

½ ounce lemon juice

¼ ounce Basic Simple Syrup
(Chapter 4)

Dash Angostura bitters

2 ounces Tomato Water
(Chapter 6)

1½ ounces vodka

GARNISH: Caprese skewer
(a small mozzarella ball and
cherry tomato wrapped in a
fresh basil leaf on a skewer)

*Food and cocktail pairings are a growing trend and this cocktail fits right in with
its garden-fresh basil, tomatoes, and mozzarella cheese. It's a truly edible cocktail!*

• • • • •

Muddle basil leaves with lemon juice and Simple Syrup. Add bitters,
Tomato Water, and vodka. Shake vigorously with ice, then strain into martini glass. Garnish with Caprese skewer.

{ Sotto Voce }

1½ ounces Solerno Blood
Orange Liqueur

¾ ounce Rhubarb and
Fennel Syrup (Chapter 4)

½ ounce freshly squeezed
lemon juice

¼ ounce Gran Classico Bitter

2 ounces soda water

GARNISH: sprig fresh dill

"Sotto voce" is a term used in music and theater to denote that the singer or speaker should lower his or her voice for the purpose of emphasizing a statement. This is a counterintuitive move, but most effective in certain dramatic situations. This beautiful pink drink acts in much the same way with its nuanced flavors quietly whispering from beneath its bold color and flash.

· · · · ·

Shake all ingredients on ice except the soda water. Strain over fresh ice in a tall glass, add soda water, and stir to combine. Garnish with a sprig of fresh dill.

{ Tea with the Bee Baron }

1½ ounces Beefeater 24 gin

¾ ounce Rooibos Tea–
Infused Honey Liqueur
(Chapter 5)

½ ounce fresh lemon juice

¼ ounce Ginger Honey Syrup
(Chapter 4)

Beefeater 24 gin has slight tea notes that work well with honey and citrus so mixing in with the Rooibos Tea–Infused Honey Liqueur is a natural fit for this cocktail. Tea, spice, honey; it just sings.

· · · · ·

Pour all ingredients into a cocktail shaker with ice. Shake well and strain into a cocktail glass.

{ Michelada }

1 glass Mexican beer
(use your favorite)

1 dash Worcestershire sauce

1 dash Tabasco sauce

½ ounce fresh lime juice

1 ounce tequila (optional)

GARNISH: Chili Salt Rim
(Chapter 6)

You may not think of using beer as an ingredient in a cocktail but this south-of-the-border refresher is one to add to your must-try list if you haven't already. Beer is a great thirst-quencher and adding a few ingredients gussies it up, adding flavor and color.

· · · · ·

Rim a tall glass with Chili Salt Rim. Fill with ice. Pour in all other ingredients. Give a little stir.

4 heaping bar spoons of avocado

Heaping pinch of cilantro

3 dime-size pieces of fresh ginger

1½ ounces Square One Cucumber Organic Vodka

1 ounce lemon juice

1 ounce pineapple juice

1 ounce agave nectar

GARNISH: wedge of lime and sprig of cilantro

This refreshing cocktail will remind you of sitting in a lounge chair by the pool. The smooth mouth feel from the avocado is sweetened by the pineapple and nectar; sharpened by ginger, spice, and cilantro; and balanced by the lemon acid. The results are surprisingly delicious!

• • • • •

Muddle the avocado, cilantro, and ginger. Add the other ingredients and shake well with ice. Double strain over fresh ice. (Makes a fabulous food pairing with cold shellfish or ceviche.)

{ Sazerac on the Rock }

2 ounces rye whiskey

½ ounce Basic Simple Syrup
(Chapter 4)

2 dashes Peychaud's Bitters

Rinse or spray of absinthe

Peychaud's Bitters Ball
(Chapter 6)

GARNISH: lemon twist
(Chapter 6)

Make this cocktail even more exciting by adding in the simple-but-brilliant twist of a Peychaud's ice ball. As the ice melts, it further flavors the drink!

. . . . .

1. Pour the rye, Basic Simple Syrup, and Peychaud's Bitters into the mixing glass and add ice to the top. Stir 20 times to chill and mix.

2. Rinse or spray the inside of a chilled rocks glass with absinthe, then drop in a Peychaud's Bitters Ball. Strain the mixture from the mixing glass over the ice ball. Twist a lemon rind over the cocktail to spray lemon oils on top, then lightly rub the rim of the glass with the oils. Set the twist on the rim of the glass.

{ The Sweetest Vice }

1½ ounces 42 Below Manuka
Honey Vodka

¾ ounce freshly squeezed
lemon juice

¾ ounce Honey Syrup
(Chapter 4)

This straight forward "sour" style cocktail comes back to the two part spirit, one part sweet, one part sour formula and highlights honey both in the spirit and the syrup, bringing a natural element to the cocktail.

• • • • •

Shake all ingredients with ice; serve in a chilled martini glass. Garnish with a lemon twist.

{ VeeVa la Vida }

4 blackberries

2 ounces Del Maguey Mezcal
Vida

½ ounce VeeV Açaí Spirit

½ ounce light agave nectar

¾ ounce lemon juice

⅛ teaspoon cayenne pepper

2 dashes each of Angostura,
Peychaud's, and mole bitters

This cocktail pairs two sustainable products—VeeV and Del Maguey Mezcal—with seasonal blackberries, lemon, cayenne, and agave nectar to create an updated drink that is inspired by classic cocktails. The balance of spicy, sweet, sour, and aromatic flavors found within the cocktail will help remind you to live life to the fullest or, as the cocktail's name suggests, VeeVa La Vida!

• • • • •

Muddle 3 blackberries in the bottom of a cocktail shaker. Pour in all other ingredients. Shake well with ice and double strain into a rocks glass filled with crushed ice. Garnish with a blackberry.

{ Damian's Diapason }

½ small apple, pitted and cut into pieces (any variety)

½ ounce Berry Shrub (Chapter 4)

½ ounce Ginger Honey Syrup (Chapter 4)

2 ounce unaged whiskey, such as White Dog

GARNISH: 3 slices fresh apple

This drink mingles fresh fruit with unique ingredients such as berry shrub and un-aged whiskey. It is an unusual drink that brings the fall harvest into the cocktail glass.

• • • • •

Muddle apple pieces, shrub, and honey syrup in a mixing glass. Add whiskey and shake with ice. Strain into a chilled cocktail glass, and garnish with apple fan (three more slices of apple fanned out).

¾ ounce pear nectar (or ¼ fresh, ripe pear that can be muddled into the cocktail glass with the lemon juice before adding the alcohol)

¼ ounce fresh lemon juice

1 ounce cachaça

½ ounce elderflower liqueur

Pinch nutmeg

2 ounces sparkling wine

Lemon twist

This sparkling cocktail is floral and fruity but not overly sweet. The floral notes in the elderflower liqueur are particularly nice with pear.

• • • • •

Shake all ingredients, except sparkling wine and lemon twist, with ice. Strain into a champagne flute, top with bubbly. Garnish with a lemon twist.

{ Tokyo Tipple }

2 lychees: 1 for muddling, 1 whole for garnish

1 ounce coconut water

¼ ounce lime juice

¾ ounce Ginger Honey Syrup (Chapter 4)

1½ ounces dry sake

Dash orange water

This cocktail is inspired by the trend of Asian influence on modern mixology. Using sake as the spirit base and coconut, which is used often in Asian cuisine, speaks to the Asian fusion cuisine that has been steaming up cocktail menus worldwide for the past decade.

· · · · ·

Muddle one lychee in the bottom of a mixing glass. Pour in all liquid ingredients, shake with ice. Strain into chilled martini glass. Garnish with whole lychee on a cocktail pick on the rim of the glass.

{ Mango Nuclear Daiquiri }

½ of a peeled, overripe mango

¾ ounce lime juice

¼ ounce Basic Simple Syrup (Chapter 4)

¼ ounce Tambourine Mountain Distillery Quandong & Gentian Bitters (substitute Angostura bitters if these are not available)

1¾ ounces Wray & Nephew Overproof Rum

GARNISH: lime wheel

This cocktail incorporates ripe mango whose natural sugar and juiciness pairs well with rum. It is sweet, strong, and easy to make. If fresh mango is not available, look for frozen mango, or create a mango purée when they are season so you can pull it out of your own freezer year round.

· · · · ·

Muddle the mango, lime juice, and Basic Simple Syrup in the bottom of a mixing glass. Add remaining ingredients and shake with ice. Double strain into a cocktail glass. Garnish with a lime wheel.

{ Golden Kiwi }

½ golden kiwi

½ ounce Basic Simple Syrup
(Chapter 4)

½ ounce lime juice

1½ ounces cachaça

Tropical fruits go well with just about any spirit because they are full of flavor and add natural sweetness to a drink. This cocktail looks and tastes particularly unique because it combines a South American spirit with a juicy and exotic golden kiwi.

· · · · ·

Muddle the kiwi with Simple Syrup and lime juice in the bottom of a mixing glass. Add cachaça and ice. Shake and double strain into a cocktail glass.

{ Never Fails Rum Punch }

½ cup fresh lime juice

½ cup raw sugar simple syrup (substitute raw sugar for white, granulated sugar in Basic Simple Syrup recipe in Chapter 4)

1 cup brewed black tea

2 cups guava juice

¼ cup freshly grated nutmeg

1 bottle spiced rum (750 ml)

Punch is the perfect party beverage because you can prepare it ahead of time and allow guests to serve themselves. Experiment with citrus, sweet syrup, tea, juices, and spirits in the proportions below and you won't go wrong when you create a punch your your guests will love.

· · · · ·

Combine all ingredients in a large punch bowl. Chill and serve.

{ Buen Provecho }

1 ounce reposado tequila

1 ounce Patron XO tequila-based coffee liqueur

½ ounce Trader Vic's Macadamia Nut Liqueur

GARNISH: jalapeño-infused whipped cream (½ ounce Jalapeño Syrup [Chapter 4] whipped with ½ cup whipping cream)

The name of this spicy-and-sweet cocktail means "bon appétit" in Spanish and makes for a scrumptious after-dinner dessert-style cocktail. There's always a little appetite left for dessert—especially a liquid one, right?

· · · · ·

Pour all liquid ingredients into a cocktail shaker. Add ice, shake vigorously, and strain into a cocktail glass. In a separate (or cleaned) shaker, vigorously shake Jalapeño Syrup and whipping cream until thick. Gently pour cream mixture over the surface of the cocktail.

INDEX

ABOUT THE AUTHOR

NATALIE BOVIS, "The Liquid Muse," is a recognized beverage consultant, mixologist, and author of *Preggatinis: Mixology for the Mom-to-Be* and *The Bubbly Bride: Your Ultimate Wedding Cocktail Guide*. She is the spokesperson for Fre® Alcohol-Removed Wine, and is launching a line of prebottled organic cocktails called OM (Organic Mixology) in 2012. She has appeared on national TV shows and regional morning shows teaching audiences how to make lip-smacking libations both with and without alcohol, and has also taught organic cocktail classes (the Liquid Muse Sustainable Sips) around the United States. While living in Los Angeles, she was often tapped to provide cocktails and Preggatinis at celebrity-studded events. Catch her weekly podcast "One for the Road" featuring chefs, mixologists, distillers, and wine makers on iTunes. She currently splits her time between Santa Fe, New Mexico and the Costa Brava in Spain. Discover more cocktail fun at *www.theliquidmuse.com*.